E. F. Babbage

The Phat Boy's Racy Description of the St. Lawrence River and its

Environs

A guide for the tourist and traveler

E. F. Babbage

The Phat Boy's Racy Description of the St. Lawrence River and its Environs
A guide for the tourist and traveler

ISBN/EAN: 9783337194499

Printed in Europe, USA, Canada, Australia, Japan

Cover: Foto ©Andreas Hilbeck / pixelio.de

More available books at **www.hansebooks.com**

THE
GRAND TRUNK
RAILWAY
—IS THE—
GREAT PLEASURE ROUTE,
—OFFERING A—

MOST ATTRACTIVE SELECTION

—OF—

POPULAR EXCURSIONS,

Via Niagara Falls, River St. Lawrence, with Thousand Islands and Rapids, Montreal, Quebec, River Saguenay, Gulf Ports, Lower Provinces, Lake Champlain, and Lake George, Saratoga, the White Mountains, etc., etc.

THE RICHELIEU AND ONTARIO NAVIGATION CO.'S STEAMERS

Comprise the original Royal Mail and Richelieu Lines, with the addition of several new steamers, thus forming two first-class Lines of Steamers, which cannot be surpassed. They are the only lines now offering Tourists an opportunity to view the MAGNIFICENT SCENERY of the THOUSAND ISLANDS, RAPIDS OF THE ST. LAWRENCE, and the far famed RIVER SAGUENAY. This Route possesses peculiar advantages over any other between Niagara Falls and Quebec. Tickets are valid by Rail or Steamer.

Pullman Palace Sleeping Cars will be attached to the evening train from Toronto, and will run through to Kingston Wharf, and passengers will remain in the car until the boat arrives. No extra charge for meals between Toronto and Montreal.

The splendid condition of the Grand Trunk Railway, including its equipment of new Passenger Cars, new Locomotives, Steel Tracks, etc., bring it prominently before the public as a first-class line, preferable to the majority between the East and West, via Gorham and Glen House, by which parties can ascend Mount Washington by carriage road, by far the best approach to this attractive mountain range.

Tickets and information may be obtained at the principal Ticket Offices, also, of the Agents of the Grand Trunk Railway Company, from whom Excursions and Tourists' Routes and Rates of Fare can be obtained.

J. B. LaBELLE, General Manager.
A. MILLOY, Traffic Manager, R. & O. N. Co.

JOSEPH HICKSON, General Manager, Grand Trunk Railway, Montreal.
W. WAINWRIGHT, Assistant   "   "   "   "   "
L. J. SEARGEANT, Traffic   "   "   "   "   "
WM. EDGAR, General Passenger Agt., "   "   "   "

THE

PHAT BOY'S RACY DESCRIPTION

——OF THE——

ST. LAWRENCE RIVER

AND ITS ENVIRONS.

A GUIDE FOR THE TOURIST AND TRAVELER.

Making a Round Trip from New York, via N. Y. C. & H. R. R. R., N. Y. W. S. & B. R. R., and the Ontario and Western R. R., to Utica, Syracuse, Rochester, Buffalo, Niagara Falls and Toronto, through Lake Ontario, Thousand Islands and Rapids of the St. Lawrence River to Montreal, Quebec, Saguenay River, Lake Champlain, Lake George, Saratoga, Albany, New York and Boston.

Fifth Edition, - - Copyrighted 1886.

E. F. BABBAGE, PUBLISHER.

ROCHESTER, N. Y.,
POST-EXPRESS PRINTING COMPANY, 12 TO 18 MILL STREET.
1886.

of compiling a book which does not contain any pictorial illustrations of the scenic beauty connected with the trip, feeling confident that a plain unvarnished description of all the various points of interest would be sufficient. The tourist can thus feast the eye on a thousand pictures that a volume ten times this size could not contain, for no matter how often you open the eyes during the day, they will fall upon some delightful scene, where the God of Nature has smiled upon her, within an hour. Neither have I given a highly colored description of the Rapids; they have been viewed and described by thousands, and the effect produced is as varied in character as the individual writers differed in temperament and looks.

Trusting that this volume may meet with as cheerful a greeting by the public as it has always accorded my efforts to please, and if its perusal causes the weary or lonesome traveler one hour of mirth or pleasure, its mission will have been accomplished.

Respectfully yours,

E. F. BABBAGE, " PHAT BOY,"

Guide to the St. Lawrence.

REFERENCES FOR THIS WORK.

We have a number of references as to the worth of this little volume. Space and time forbid a mention of them all; some of the most prominent will suffice:

1. At the request of a friend I purchased a copy of the Phat Boy's Racy description of the St. Lawrence River and the perusal caused me to laugh so much that the corners of my mouth shook hands at the back of my neck.

T. W. O'BRIEN.

2. At Alexandria Bay last season, a lady had the misfortune to sprain her ankle, (no matter how; but we will say, least some one may be led astray as to the real cause, that it was not done falling or stumbling over the editor.) We very kindly gave her a copy of the "Phat Boy's" Racy Description of the St. Lawrence River, and she was able to walk in ten hours after the accident, apparently as well as ever.

3. This volume will not bring home a stray cow; but it will do the next best thing; milk them in the pasture, thus saving the wear and tear incident to their coming home.

4. The delight and pleasure that the perusal of your little volume gave me, I am unable to Express.—SUSAN B.

N. B.—Then send it by Freight.—" PHAT BOY."

5. A lady who had one copy (by the way, she was married,) wrote for the second; it was sent to her; but mean-

while she had changed her residence to the Lunatic Asylum. Now here is a chance for married men who wish to become single for 25 cents. Send for a copy.

6. A very restless, nervous man bought a copy; read to page 63, went to sleep quietly for ten hours. First good rest in four years.

7. It is good for maiden ladies; has been known to cure headache, toothache, sprains, bruises, ingrowing nails, and it matters not.

8. Eli Perkins will read a copy of this work, August 25th, 1886, and from that day until death will speak the truth.

"PHAT BOY'S" RACY DESCRIPTION

—OF—

THE ST. LAWRENCE RIVER.

THE St. Lawrence River, with its Thousand Islands and Rapids, is day by day attracting more and more attention among tourists. There is so much that is grand, weird, sublime and exhilerating in the scenery and balmy atmosphere of the majestic river, as it passes in its onward flow from the lake to the gulf, that we need not for a moment wonder why it is that there is a great annual increase in the number of those intelligent people, who, from East, West and South, repair to its placid waters in summer to recuperate their wasted energies and enjoy that luxuriating season known to every American as "vacation."

A vacation on the St. Lawrence, means a sojourn at some pretentious or lowly cottage, or at some hotel of either class for a few days, or for one, two or more weeks, as the time, finances and inclination of the individual may dictate; or it may, as in hundreds of instances it does, only include a voyage of rapid transit from New York to Utica, Clayton, Niagara Falls, Lewiston, Toronto or Kingston to Alexandria Bay or Montreal, then return home. There are several different popular starting places to reach the river; it is presumed you will take the most convenient one, and we will consider ourselves pleased with the selection.

ROUTE A.

NEW YORK CENTRAL & H. R. R. R. LESSEES OF THE WEST SHORE ROUTE.

THE TOURIST ROUTE OF THE NORTH.

While many suppose that both sides of the Hudson River present equal attraction—and it would be hard to decide which is the most beautiful—it is a curious fact that all, or nearly all, the noted summer resorts for which the country adjacent is famous are located on its western bank. Thus, starting from New York and following up the West Shore Route, we find the Palisades, Tappan, Rockland Lake, Stony Point, Cranston's, West Point, Cornwall, Lakes Mohonk and Minnewaska, the Catskills, Saratoga, Mount McGregor, and the Adirondacks (in which the great river rises), all on the same side, and all easily accessible by the New York, West Shore and Buffalo Railway. In addition to these, the magnificent cars of this route convey the traveler to Lake George, Lake Champlain and Montreal, on the north; Sharon Springs, Cooperstown, Richfield Springs, Niagara Falls, Buffalo and Chautauqua Lake, and make close connections for all the White Mountain and Eastern resorts, for the Thousand Islands, Watkin's Glen and the Lake region of Central New York. It is thus emphatically the tourists route of the north, and realizing this fact, its projectors and managers have done everything in their power to render it attractive to this constantly increasing and most fastidious class of travelers.

While traversing the most picturesque portions of a State noted for its scenery, this railway is the most complete in all details of construction and equipment of any in this country. It is a double track, steel rail line, with an unusually wide space between tracks, running north from Jersey City along the west shore of the Hudson to Albany, and thence through the fertile Valley of the Mohawk and across Central New York, touching at Utica, Syracuse and Rochester, to Buffalo and Niagara Falls. Its grades are easy, its curves are light, its steel rails are among the heaviest known in railway construction, and its road-bed will be crowned with a deep ballasting of stone.

Owing to this excellent road-bed and the great strength of its iron bridges this company has been able to build exceptionally heavy locomotives for its various classes of traffic. The passenger engines burn anthracite coal, and are designed to haul trains of from ten to fifteen coaches at a high rate of speed. They are provided with special arrangements in the fire and smoke boxes and smoke stacks to consume all gases, and prevent the escape of smoke or cinders.

LOCOMOTIVES, CARS AND STATION HOUSES.

The entire passenger equipment of the road was especially designed and built by the Pullman Palace Car Company, and is the most complete in all details pertaining to elegance of finish, comfort and safety in the world. From the palatial buffet cars with interiors finished in variegated hard-woods and furnished with plate glass mirrors, luxurious arm chairs, soft carpets and rich drapery, to the smoking cars, finished with figured oak, and provided with revolving chairs, upholstered in leather, all are the most perfect specimens of the car-builder's art extant. The exterior of the cars making up West Shore passenger trains is painted in a rich dark olive and gold, which produces a most pleasing effect.

The station houses erected along the entire route from New York to Buffalo are architectural gems, harmonious in color and design with the beautiful and picturesque scenery through which the road passes. Those at the New York terminus, at Kingston, Albany, Utica, Syracuse and Buffalo will, when finished, surpass in completeness and artistic design any series of railway stations ever erected by a single company.

THE NEW YORK STATION.

The New York terminus of this great railway was projected upon a scale of vastness and perfection of detail commensurate with the rest of the magnificent scheme. It is at Weehawken, opposite the heart of the great city, and close beneath the height on which Alexander Hamilton fell before the pistol of Aaron Burr. It extends for more than a mile along the river front, and, with its numerous docks and piers, presents nearly six miles of working space, in which vessels of every description may receive freight. From here commodious and elegantly appointed ferry-boats run to the handsome up-town passenger station at the foot of Forty-second Street. The express trains of the West Shore Route leave from and arrive at the down town station, foot of Jay Street, accessible from Elevated stations at Franklin, Chambers and Barclay Streets; also leave from and arrive at the up town station at the foot of West 42nd Street, New York, and from the foot of Fulton Street, Brooklyn. The passenger from New York has thus an option of starting from any one of half a dozen points, a great convenience when one considers the peculiar position and length of the city. Passengers are cautioned to consult official time-tables in the Company's publications, or in the leading newspapers, with the view of ascertaining just what trains leave from and arrive at the various stations named.

In the subsequent pages one may obtain partial glimpses of some of the innumerable delightful places to which this highway for business and pleasure travel will guide him, and a few hints of the many pleasures in store for his summer holiday.

BETWEEN NEW YORK AND THE THOUSAND ISLANDS.

"THE ONTARIO ROUTE."

New York, Ontario & Western Railway Co.

Running from New York to the City of Oswego, on Lake Ontario, and in connection with the R. W. & O. R. R. from Cape Vincent, forming the most attractive route to the St. Lawrence River. It is the only line running Pullman sleepers through without change between New York and the Thousand Islands. On arrival of trains at Cape

Vincent, the new steamer St. Lawrence, the handsomest and swiftest on the River, leaves for all landings among the Islands.

The train carrying through sleepers leaves New York at 5:30 p. m., arriving at Cape Vincent at 9:30 a. m., and Alexandria Bay at 11:30 a m.; giving tourists a delightful ride of twenty-five miles down the Islands to the Bay. Ample time is given at Richland for breakfast. Returning, the St. Lawrence leaves Alexandria Bay at 4:00 p. m., arriving at Cape Vincent at 6:00 p. m., and train leaves at 6:10 p. m., arriving in New York at 9:30 a. m.

The depots and ferries of the New York, Ontario & Western Railway are located in New York at the foot of West 42nd Street and Harrison Street, from which points commodious and elegantly appointed ferry boats run to the passenger station at Weehawken, and in Brooklyn at the foot of Fulton, Brooklyn Annex.

The route of the Ontario and Western, after leaving Weehawken, is west of the Palisades, through the counties of Bergen in New Jersey, and Rockland in New York, following the fertile and romantic valley of the Hackensack. At Valley Cottage the road tunnels through the mountains, and for sixteen miles skirts the banks of the Hudson, through the Highlands, traversing all the historic and picturesque points along that world-famed stream. Then over the foot-hills of the Catskills, through the mountains of Central New York, and along the valleys of the Delaware, Neversink, Beaverkill and Chenango Rivers, with their lovely picturesque views of mountain, lake and river, to Lake Ontario, making one of the most beautiful routes across the Empire State.

The night express trains run every day, including Sunday. The Pullman buffet sleepers are of the latest models, and complete in all details pertaining to elegance of finish, comfort and safety.

The City of Kingston, Ontario, is easily reached from Cape Vincent via Steamer Maud, which leaves after the arrival of train from New York, and returning leaves in the afternoon, connecting with train for the south.

The New York Central & Hudson River R. R., leaving the Grand Central Depot, 42nd Street, New York, passes along the beautiful Hudson River to Albany, then the great four tracked railroad of the world conveys you to Utica (where the direct connections are made with the Utica & Black River R. R.; then the traveler can, if he desires pass over this popular route, reaching in a few hours the majestic St. Lawrence at Clayton, connecting with the steamers of the Richelieu and Ontario Navigation Company direct for Montreal), Syracuse, Rochester, Buffalo, or

NIAGARA FALLS.

The ticket office of the Grand Trunk R. R. and Richelieu and Ontario Navigation Company Royal Mail Line is located at No. 4, International Hotel, and is presided over by Mrs. L. Barber, who will cheerfully give you any information desired. Trains leave the Falls every morning, Sunday excepted, by Grand Trunk R. R. to Toronto, and arrive in time to connect with Mail Line for Montreal. Trains leave Niagara Falls every morning except Sunday, at 9:05 a. m., via Central Hudson Branch for Lewiston, where con-

THE
CLIFTON HOUSE,
NIAGARA FALLS.

FRONTING THE STATE AND CANADIAN RESERVATIONS.

THE CLIFTON

Is the ONLY Hotel from the apartments and verandahs of which there is

A Full and Unobstructed View of the Falls,

a fact visitors should bear in mind.

The view includes the Islands, Rapids and Adjacent Country for Miles.

Niagara has the endorsement of the Medical and Sanitary authorities, for health, invigorating air and salubrity of climate, at all seasons, and is delightfully cool during the Summer months.

The Hotel is elegant in all features and apartments; has apartments *en suite*, with every convenience and luxury, and the *cuisine* and service is in all particulars superior.

Address, for all information, by mail or telegraph,

GEORGE M. COLBORN,
Niagara Falls, N. Y.

nections are made with the fast sailing side-wheel steamboat

CHICORA,

crossing the beautiful Lake Ontario and arriving in Toronto in time to connect with Richelieu and Ontario Navigation Company Royal Mail Line for Kingston, Alexandria Bay, Thousand Islands and Rapids of the St. Lawrence River to Montreal.

" THANK GOD " NIAGARA FALLS IS FREE.—BORN AGAIN.

From the first issue of this little volume up to the present I have labored to inform the public regarding the many schemes and extortions at the Falls; been the only champion of fifty millions of people, and with my coat off and sleeves rolled up, worked for the passage of the bill to make Niagara Falls free. Now, that success has perched upon our banners, we propose to put the people of Niagara Falls upon the stool of repentance on their good behavior as it were for the season of 1885-6. After that time, should they merit kind treatment or praise I shall be most happy to say so. If, on the other hand, they deserve censure for any device or schemes to entrap the stranger or visitor, I shall ventilate it, and, as in the past, handle them without gloves.

Hoping the dear public will sanction the charity I have displayed and post me regarding their treatment at the Falls the coming season, I am Respectfully Yours.

E. F. BABBAGE, "Phat Boy,"
21 Chestnut Park Rochester, N. Y.

N. B.—From the above request to my friends I received during 1885 as complaints, five letters. No. 1 contained the complaint of an abuse that does not exist at present. I was at the Falls June 2d and 3d, 1886, and know that the Select men of the village with the aid of the Superintendent of the Park for the State, (a most worthy official) have taken hold of and crushed out the above. As the above does not continue there is no need to mention it. No. 2 complaint was charges at a certain hotel. If I hear any more will ventilate it. No. 3 would not have been written if the parties had been located at the Clifton House. Nos. 4 and 5 were complaints regarding the Indian stores and curiosity shops, over which I have no control, and for which fact I am thankful, as there are so many of them good, bad, and indifferent, I have no doubt it would be just the same in any large city city where any branch of trade was carried on by the same number of people. Respectfully Yours,

E. F. B.

As many of the tourists leave Niagara Falls in the morning at 9:05 o'clock by rail to Lewiston, and connect with the Steamer Chicora, for Toronto, I will mention the places and points.

LEWISTON.

This village is situated at the head of navigation, on the Lower Niagara, and is a place of considerable importance. It lies three miles below Devil's Hole, and seven miles below the Falls. Lewiston is a pleasant, well built village, but its commercial prospects have been very much injured by the construction of the Erie and Welland Canals.

QUEENSTON

is a small village situated nearly opposite to Lewiston, and contains about 350 inhabitants. It is associated in history with the gallant defence made by the British on the adjacent heights in the war of 1812. The village is pleasantly situated, but has suffered from the same causes that have retarded the growth of Lewiston. The river here becomes more tranquil, the shores less broken and wild, and the change in the scenery affords a pleasing transition from the sublime to the beautiful.

BROCK'S MONUMENT.

The monument stands on the Heights of Queenston, from whence the village derives its name. The present structure occupies the site of the former one, which was blown up by some miscreant on the 17th of April, 1840. The whole edifice is 185 feet high; on the sub-base, which is 40 feet square and 30 feet high, are placed four lions, facing North, South, East and West; the base of the pedestal is $21\frac{1}{2}$ feet square and 10 feet high; the pedestal itself is 16 feet square and 10 feet high, surmounted by a heavy cornice, ornamented with lions' heads and wreaths in altro relievo. In ascending from the top of the pedestal to the top of the base of the shaft, the form changes from square to round. The shaft is a fluted column of free-stone, 75 feet high and 10 feet in diameter, on which stands a Corinthian capital 10 feet high, whereon is wrought, in relief, a statue of the Goddess of War. On this capital is the dome 9 feet high, reached by 250 spiral steps from the base on the inside. On the top of the dome is placed a colossal statue of General Brock.

THE ROSSIN HOUSE,

TORONTO

Remodeled and Refurnished.

NEW PLUMBING THROUGHOUT.

The Most Complete, Luxurious, and Liberally Managed Hotel in Ontario.

Immunity from noxious gases and malaria guaranteed by the most perfect system of ventilation, traps and thorough plumbing known to sanitary science.

MARK H. IRISH,
HENRY J. NOLAN,   Proprietor,
Chief Clerk.

called York. Toronto bay is a beautiful inlet, separated from the main body of Lake Ontario, except at its entrance, by a long, narrow sandy beach. The South-Western extremity is called Gibraltar Point. It is 165 miles from Kingston, 45 miles from Hamilton, and 50 miles from the falls of Niagara. The population in 1717 was 1,200; but at the present time it amounts to about 75,000. The city is laid out at right angles. Its chief public buildings are the cathedrals and churches, the Parliament House, University of Toronto, Trinity College, Normal School, St. Michael's College, Osgoode Hall, St. Lawrence Hall, Mechanics Institute, Provincial Lunatic Asylum, Post-Office, Exchange and City Schools. Its system of free public schools is one of the most perfect and best conducted in America. Among the many pleasant drives around this city the traveler should visit College Avenue and the Queen's Park. In this park is erected a statue of the Queen and a monument to commemorate the college youths who fell at Ridgeway defending the country from the attacks of the Fenians. The University of Toronto, a most magnificent building, is also situated in this park. The Parliament of Ontario and the principal law courts are held in this city. It is connected by the Grand Trunk Railway and steamboats from all points. The two largest hotels in Toronto are the Rossin House and the Queens Hotel. These hotels have every modern improvement and the prices are graduated according to the location of room. If carriages are needed while in the city Telephone No. 109, R. Bond's Livery, who has everything first class in the carriage line, " A 1."

PORT HOPE

is situated 65 miles from Toronto. A small stream, which here falls into the lake, has formed a valley, in which the town is located. The harbor at the mouth of this stream is shallow, but safe and commodious. Port Hope is a pretty town; on the western side the hills rise gradually one above the other. The highest summit, called "Fort Orton," affords a fine prospect, and overlooks the country for a great distance. The village is incorporated; population about 5,114. A direct route to Rochester by the Steamer Norseman leaves this port every morning, except on Sunday, calling at Port Hope and connecting with Grand Trunk train from Toronto every week day morning and arriving in Rochester the same afternoon. The Grand Summer Excursions of the Norseman from Rochester to Alexandria Bay leaving Rochester every Saturday evening and passing through the 1,000 Island scenery of the St. Lawrence River arriving at Alexandria Bay in time for dinner, giving the passengers about five hours at the Bay and returning to Rochester early on Monday. I have advised many of my friends to make this trip, all of which have expressed themselves as delighted.

COBOURG,

seven miles below Port Hope, contains 6,000 inhabitants. It has seven churches, two banks, three grist mills, two founderies, and the largest cloth factory in the Province. It is also the seat of Victoria College and Theological Institute. Midway between Port Hope and Cobourg is "Duck Island," on which a light house is maintained by the government.

FOR THE BENEFIT OF ALL,

we submit the following time-table—not forgetting to mention that steamboats are not infallible, but are governed by man, accompanied by steam, wind and water. If the boat is one hour late in starting from any given point, it is likely she will remain so, as I know of but one boat in the line that can beat or surpass schedule time.

LEAVING EVERY DAY—SUNDAYS EXCEPTED.

Toronto (Sunday Excepted)........	2:00 P. M.	Morrisburg................ ......12:05	P. M.
Kingston (Monday Excepted)............	5:00 A. M.	Chrysler's Farm..........12:17	"
		Aultsville....................12:30	"
		Farren's Point............12:40	"
Clayton	6:00 "	Dickenson's Landing....12:55	"
Alexandria Bay	7:00 "	Long Sault...... .... 1:00	"
Brockville..........	9:30 "	Last of U. S. shore....... 1:15	"
Prescott 10:30	"	Cornwall....... .... 1:30	"
Galop Rapids 11:05	"	Coteau Landing.......... 4:00	"
Iroquois...................11:35	"	Cedar Rapid.............. 4:30	"
Narrowest Point 11:45	"	Indian Pilot............... 6:00	"
Rapid Platt.... ....11:55	"	Montreal 7:00	"

We assume that we are now fairly entering on the majestic stream on the Canadian side, having left Lake Ontario and entered the St. Lawrence River, our first landing will be at

THE CITY OF KINGSTON,

which has a population of 15,000, was founded in 1672, by Governor DeCourcelles, receiving the name of Fort Cataraqui. Later, a massive stone fort was built by Count De Frontenac, and received his name. In 1762 the place was taken by the British, who gave it its present name. As a place of defense it stands next in strength to Quebec. The batteries of Fort Henry are calculated for the reception of numerous cannon and mortars of the largest calibre. These, together with neighboring martello towers, form a formidable defense against any aggressive movement which might be directed against the city. These fortifications are seen to excellent advantage from the steamer soon after it leaves the dock.

On the right is Garden Island; on the left, Cedar Island, and behind is Fort Henry. There is here, also, in view, the round stone towers referred to above. Near the middle of the river is Wolf, or Long Island, 21 miles long, and 7 miles wide near the Western end. There is nothing either of romance or historical episode to weave into our story, concerning the inhabitants of this, the largest of the Thousand Island group. Suffice it to say, that the territory is a portion of the Dominion of Canada, and that the habits of civilized life characterize the people. Between one channel and the main land there is St. John's or Howe Island, of no mean proportions.

Ordinarily, we have now spent about one hour on the steamer from Kingston, and come to the point in the channel where we must diverge either for Gananoque or Clayton. We are bound for Clayton and the American channel of the St. Lawrence River. (For description of Gananoque and the Canadian channel. see Route of the Island Wanderer, old page 38.) As soon as the light-house on Burnt Island comes in view, we may be said to have fairly entered upon the real beauty of the "sacred river of America." Between here and Gananoque we pass many pretty little isles of six or eight acres. On the right is a range light, the boat of course, passing between the two. It is said that from the deck of the steamer, one hundred islands can be counted—in fact, the panorama is probably matchless on the globe. While the islands are so numerous both on the right and left, the boat glides by without allowing the tourist to be distracted with the rapture of delight that is feasting his eyes. Some of these isles are scarcely more than barren rocks, while others are paradises of verdure.

For the first three quarters of an hour after leaving Kingston, there is nothing especially worthy of note. Then we strike the cross-over channel. Now, the time is early morning, the sun is quite bright, and the atmosphere is remarkably clear. The scene is now attractive. Look ahead in the distance a little to the left, and you will behold the eagle tree. Hundreds have been deceived with the idea that it was an actual live eagle, spreading its wings and soaring aloft to a height that the imagination can scarcely reach. It is a delusion; 'tis nothing but a tree, as its true features, or rather beautiful foliage has deceived the eye of the novice of this region.

On the left is Grindstone Island. On it is an organized community. The inhabitants are farmers, and for the education of whose children a school is maintained.

It may be well to state here that authorities (?) differ as to how many islands there really are. Some say fifteen hundred; some eighteen hundred, and others carefully write, *nearly* two thousand. Life is too short for us to stop and count these natural beauties, and even the pilots have no desire to earn fame as statisticians by asserting the correct number. The " Phat Boy " has just issued the only correct

map of the St. Lawrence River, published, which will not be misleading to the student of minute details. But we digress.

"DO YOU GO OUT FISHING?"

Well not often, you see this ponderous body of mine does not fit the average fishing boat. My fears are not all bound up in that one fact, nor in the satisfaction that if the boat should upset that I would not sink, but the fear that is indelibly printed upon my mind, that, as I would float, and being so large, some steamboat captain or pilot would take me for an island, lay alongside and let the passengers off for a little pic-nic or an hour's pleasure. Think of it.

"NOT A GEORGE WASH."

He had told several very improbable stories bordering upon the Eli Perkins order and then remarked to a friend that he could not tell a lie. But the friend replied, that he could the moment he heard it, and to the best of his judgment he had told several.

Names of Islands that are numbered on the Phat Boy's Birdseye Chart of the St. Lawrence, because the space would not permit printing the names in full :

53.	Robinson,	60.	Devil's Oven,
54.	Calumet,	61.	Cherry,
56.	Seven.	$61\frac{1}{2}$.	Southgate, R. H.,
57.	Pratt,	62.	Pullman.
58.	Wau Winnet,	63.	Nobby.
59.	Cuba,	64.	Welcome,

65.	Friendly,	109.	Rattle Snake,
66.	Florence,	111.	Round,
67.	Linlith Gow, late Maud,	112.	Poverty.
68.	Imperial,	114.	Hemlock,
70.	Resort,	115.	Snipe,
71.	Deshler,	116.	Three Brothers,
72.	Kipp,	117.	Half Way,
73.	Terry,	137.	Brush,
75.	Judge Donahue,	139.	Flat,
79.	Proctor,	141.	Round Top,
80.	Pike,	142.	Indian Chief,
81.	Idlewild,	143.	Pine Tree,
82.	Little Lehigh,	144.	Middle,
83.	Sport,	145.	Big,
84. 85.	} Summer Land Group,	146. 147.	Shoemakers, Bill Berry,
86.	Arcada,	148.	Raspberry,
88.	Schooner,	149.	Bush,
94.	Snake,	150.	Coles and Smith,
95.	Float,	151.	H. A. Fields,
96.	Milk,	160.	Melville,
97.	Sugar,	163.	Dixon,
100.	Wallace,	164.	McGraw,
101.	Walton Lotis' Land,	165.	Sears,
102.	Deer,	166.	Benedict,
107.	Hoopers,	167.	Ruycraft,
108.	Shanter,	169.	Deniston.

Having already intimated that there are other routes which lead to the point in the river which we have now reached, we return westward to bring another party through the American channel.

YOU KNOW HER.

She is one of the strong minded of the female sex, and generally has her own way in everything. At any rate she stands ready at any and all times to combat with any one of the lords of creation, or otherwise, who may dispute her sway. We prefer your imagination to fill in as a description, because it would be next to an impossibility for me to. She has all the requisites : the thin, tall figure, the hatchet face, sharp nose, wears glasses, and always carries an umbrella. About one each day will pass down this route in Summer, except when an Eastern or Western Excursion comes ; then it will be hard to select those who are not of her kind. The first object that strikes the eye is our manly figure. After looking it well over, she remembers that fat people are proverbially jolly and good natured, so she breaks into conversation, and about the first question she asks is : "Were you always as large as you are now ?" " Oh! Yes. I was born this size." The answer causes her to discover she has left out the word "proportion." So she apologizes, smiles for the first time, and we are friends for the trip.

CLAYTON

is in the American channel. In the distant front, just before landing, we have a magnificent view of Prospect Park and hill, a delightful spot for recreation and pleasure. No better view can be had of the islands and surrounding country than from the eminence of the hill. Clayton is our first stopping place. It is a village that derives its importance to tourists as being the terminus of the Utica and Black River Railroad, and here it is where passengers from the East generally get their first glimpse of the St. Lawrence. There are three good hotels, the Hubbard, Walton and The West End Hotels, kept by as genial landlords as ever lived, and from the town many fishing parties go out daily. The steamer J. F. Maynard runs from this port in connection with the above named railroads for Alexandria Bay and other landing places *en route*. Opposite Clayton, on the left as we proceed down the river, is Governor Island, owned by Hon. Thomas. G. Alvord, of Syracuse. Next to Gov. Alvord's Isle on left is Calumet, five acres, owned by Chas. G. Emery, of Old Judge cigarette and tobacco fame, who has lavishly expended a large amount of money for comfort. His villa and apartments are quite striking, having 1,000 feet of dockage and a stone wall all around the island, 4,300 feet—the only island having an elevation of 35 feet and a perfect soil, all productive. He purchased the steam yacht Calumet, said to be the fastest yacht on the river. The next island on the left, about 200 yards distant, is Powder Horn. The origin of this "euphonious" name has not been handed down by tradition. On the right is Washington Island; on the left, nearly opposite, is Bluff Island, and behind which is Robin's Island. Next, on the right, over two miles from Clayton, is

ROUND ISLAND

and park. This is the property of the Baptist Association, and every year people of this persuasion in large numbers gather for religious worship and recreation. There is a temperance hotel, fitted with the modern appointments, for the accommodation of 300 guests, named the Round Island House. The docks are in excellent condition, and the fishing boats are favorites. On the left is Little Round Island, and "Hog's Back." We have now several cottages in view; the one painted dark brown is owned by Mr. Harbodle. On the point is Ethelridge cottage, and many others not known to me, as they spring up as quickly as mushrooms do in an open field.

Leaving Round Island, and looking in the distant front, we have a view of the Thousand Island Park. About one mile from Round Island, on the right, is Watch Island or "Indolence," owned by S. T. Skinner. On the left are Bluff, Maple and Hemlock, the three pretty islands fronting the foot of Grindstone Island. On Hemlock is the Cliff House, owned by Mr. Garrison, of Syracuse. About five minutes after leaving Round Island, we come in sight of Hub Island and House, burned in March, 1884, which lie on the left; Grinnell's Island and House; Otsego Camp is also on the left. On the right is Fisher's landing, Robinson's island, owned by Eugene Robinson, New York banker and broker (he broke Drew), Johnson's Light, Washburn Island and Frederick Island. Mr. Johnson, the original lighthouse keeper, and after whom the island is named, was the man who burned the Robert Peel, the English vessel, in retaliation for sending the Carolina over Niagara Falls.

Just before landing at Thousand Island Park, upper end of Well's Island, now called Wellesley Island, is Twin Island, owned by J. L. Huntington. On the left, and in connection with the Thousand Island Park, is the bath house, in a dilapidated condition, where the Methodists can get baptism, *a la* Bob Ingersoll, with soap. Said to be good for this world, if not hereafter. We now land at

THOUSAND ISLAND PARK.

The boat stops at the Western End of Wells Island, at a fine wharf, and close to a large number of handsome cottages. You can tell what the place is the moment you approach it. There is no mistaking a Methodist Summer Camp, find it where you will. It is always neat and clean and orderly. This is the Thousand Island Park, a Methodist resort, opened in 1873. Although the scenery is somewhat marred by the great number of solemn-faced clergymen strolling about the grounds, it is still one of the most beautiful spots to be found among the islands. Camp-meetings are held here ; also Sunday-school and temperance and educational conventions, and other meetings all through the summer. A large and spacious hotel, completed, was opened July 10th, 1883. The name was originally Thousand Island Camp Ground, but was changed in 1878 to its present name.

Again on our way, the first house on the left is owned by Harlow J. Remington, Ilion, whose fame and fortune is in rifles. Next on the left is Wellesley House and beautiful cottage. On the right, handsome villas line the shore of the island. About half a mile from Wellesley House is Jolly Oak Point, with its four cottages, two owned by the Norton brothers, a third by Dr. Ferguson, and the fourth by Hon. W. W. Butterfield, of Redwood. From here to Lookout Point is about half a mile ; and next is Rood's place, with a fine dock and good accommodations for tourists. About two hundred yards below is Peel's dock, where the boat Robert Peel was burned in 1837. This dock was rebuilt in 1884. Robin's cottage, 100 feet to the left ; a little below on the right is the farm of Captain Jack; you can see the old saw mill in a dilapidated condition on the bank. Opposite on the left is the celebrated Limburger cheese factory. (Post mortem examinations held here weekly.) (This "goak" would take better if you was just introduced to Limburger for the first time.) On the right is Collins' dock; below a few feet is Calumet Island and cottage, owned by Rev. Henry G. Waite, of Ilion, N. Y. On the right lies the remains of old Captain Jack's boat, gone to rest. * * * Here you are expected to drop a tear. Brown's Bay on the left and Swan Bay on the right. The next island on the right is owned by Mr. Moffet, of Watertown, N. Y. Passing the bays, we come on the right to Central Park, formerly Grinnell's Point and parade ground, purchased by parties and laid out for a park. Several large and beautiful cottages were built last season and many contemplated for this season. Foot of Central Park is Page Point, a former wood station for the N. T. Co.'s line of steamers. On the right is

POINT VIVIAN.

Point Vivian is situated on the main shore of the St. Lawrence River, about $2\frac{1}{2}$ miles from Alexandria Bay. It was formerly owned by Capt. W. H. Houghton, and was purchased by Messrs. Geo. Ivers, John J. Kinney, Isaac A. Wood, Dr. L. E. Jones, R. Barnes, Rezot Tozer and E. Hungerford, in the fall of 1877 (all of Evans Mills, N. Y.) They had it surveyed into forty building lots, with parks, avenues and streets. A magnificent dock was built 200 feet long, and any boat from a skiff to an ocean steamer can land here.

Point Vivian is one of the pleasantest resorts on the river; here every one throws off all business cares, sitting under the wide spreading branches of the fragrant pine, watching sail and steam crafts passing up or down this beautiful queen of rivers. It is situated in what is known as the narrows and is noted for its fine fishing grounds. The boss fisherman on the point is Tozer. He appears to have a charm (we don't know where, but we know he has one), and when he launches his barque the fish swarm around and just ask to be " tuk in," and are always took.

The following named persons together with the original purchasers have built cottages here :

R. Rodenhurst, Theresa, N. Y.
Mrs. Chadwick, Theresa, N. Y.
C. Allen, Theresa, N. Y.
Sidney Cooper, Watertown, N. Y.
C. Young, Syracuse, N. Y..
L. Sharon, Sterlingville, N. Y.
Mr. Aldrich, Sterlingville, N. Y.
M. Horton, Watertown, N. Y.
Taylor, Watertown, N. Y.
W. S. Cooper, Evans Mills.
E. O. Hungerford, Evans Mills.
A. M. Cook, Evans Mills.
C. Briant, Evans Mills.
E. Hungerford, Evans Mills.
Whitney & Kinney, Gouverneur.
L. Smith, Gouverneur.

Several gentlemen from Watertown have purchased a number of lots adjoining and have been incorporated with the point. The management intends to add some valuable improvements the coming season, grading the streets and avenues, building a large ice house, putting up wind mill, &c. There are a few more desirable lots for sale on this point, those contemplating building on the river would do well to visit this famous resort. Connected with this point is

LONG POINT,

owned by Mr. Curtis of Cleveland, Ohio. He has erected a nice cottage thereon, where he spends his summer. Curtis is a "prince of good fellows," and the pointers reckon on him as one of 'em.

The officers are:

W. S. Cooper, President.

Sidney Cooper, R. Rodenhurst, John J. Kinney, Trustees.

W. M. Comstock, Secretary.

Opposite Point Vivian on the left is Island Royal, owned by Royal E. Deane, of New York, firm of Bramall, Deane & Co. Mr. Deane is a very enthusiastic lover of the scenery as well as the hunting and fishing in this vicinity, coming to this, his summer home, quite early in the spring, and often remaining until winter fairly sets in, for no where else can he get such a variety of fish and game and have the surroundings so agreeable.

After leaving point Vivian, on the right, is Curtis Point and cottage. The next is Alleghaney Point, owned by J. S. Laney, of Pittsburg, Pa. The fence was built to keep the children from falling into the river. Next on the right is Keppler Point, Beula Vista Lodge, owned by F. A. Bosworth, of Milwaukee, Wis. He is an invalid, and has not been home for ten years, says he will not return home until he can walk. I am pleased to say he told a friend of mine that his stay of three months here was of more benefit to him than a tour through Europe. He died in 1885. Centennial Isle is owned by Mr. Sissons, of Watertown, N. Y. Comfort, in close proximity is owned by A. S Clark, of the Chicago, Ill., Board of Trade. His is the largest and finest cottage of the group. Beyond is Hills Island, also Devil's Rock and Oven. This gentleman has expended a large amount of money in building a stone wall around the same, and in many ways beautifying the surroundings. On the left is Winslow Point and Seven Isles. Beyond is Louisiana Point owned by Judge La Batte, of New Orleans. Next on the right is Warner's Isle, very much on the dilapidated order. On the right is Cuba Isle, owned by W. F. Storey, of Buffalo, N. Y. A little further on is Edgewood Park, owned by a Cleveland Stock Company, who contemplate many changes the coming season, and Edgewood Cottage, owned by G. C. Martin of Watertown, N. Y. Next on the right is Cherry Isle, upon which are erected several cottages, one is owned by Rev. George Rockwell, of Fulton, N. Y., and occupied by Mr. Easton and family, of Brooklyn, N. Y.; he was the first pastor of the Reformed Church of Alexandria Bay. The two large cottages are owned by A. B. Pullman, and G. B. Marsh, of Chicago, Ill.,—named Ingleside and Melrose Lodge. Here the Hon. John A. Logan and wife were entertained for several days in 1885. Opposite on the left is Pullman, Nobby, Friendly, Rye, Welcome, Florence, Imperial and Linlith Gow. This group may be seen in the order given, beyond is Westminster Park, Hart's Island, Fairy Land and Dishler. We now shoot into Alexandria Bay.

Cherry Island is owned by Rev. George Rockwell and occupied by Mr. J. T. Easton, of Brooklyn, N. Y. Next island on left, Devil's Rock and Oven; a little beyond is Cuba, owned by W. S. Story, of Buffalo; a little above on the left is Wau Winnet, owned by Mr. Hill, of Chicago, Ill. Next, on the left, we pass very close to Warner's Isle (a little dilapidated). The next above, about three hundred feet, is Comfort Isle, owned by A. E. Clark, of the Chicago Produce Exchange. Neh-Mahbin joins Comfort by a bridge. On the right is Louisiana Point, owned by Judge La Batte, of New Orleans, La., who died about one year ago. A little above, on the left, is Keepler Point and cottage; a little above is Brown's Bay; a little above, on the left, Alleghany Point and cottage, owned by Mr. Lahney, of Pittsburg, Pa.; a little above, on the left, is Curtis Point and cottage, owned by Mr. Curtis, of Cleveland, Ohio. A bridge connects him with ex-Mayor Rose's Island, who has just built a very handsome cottage and dock. Next on the left is Point Vivian; beyond is Brown's cottage; opposite, on the right, is Island Royal, owned by Royal E. Deane, of New York. The next island has always been a favorite place for campers. Nothing right or left for about one mile. We then arrive at Central Park, which has very many beautiful cottages and hotel. Island head of Central Park is owned by Mr. Moffatt, of Watertown; opposite, on the right, is Palisade Point and handsome cottage—a great point for campers. After leaving the Bay, on the left is a cottage owned by Mr. Webb. A little beyond, on the left, is Capt. Jack's farm-house and old mill; opposite is Limburger cheese factory (we do not get close enough to interfere with your sense of smell; keep your seat). Opposite is a brown cottage and bridge; a little farther on is a farm and house; on the right is Lookout Point and cottage. The barns look as if some thrifty and prosperous farmer resided there. Just beyond is Jolly Oaks and its four cottages; Sans Souci and others, with camping parties, line the shore until we come to Wellsley House; on the left is Fisher's Landing, Cedar, Hemlock and Robinson's Island, on the left beyond which is Johnson's light and cottage; a little beyond is Thousand Island Park, with its magnificent hotel, hundreds of cottages boats and boat-houses. This is run by the Methodists. In the distance front, on the left, is Round Island Hotel, and splendid villas line the banks all round the island, which is owned by the Baptist's Association. In the distance is Clayton, in front of which is Gouverner's Island, owned by Gov. Alvord, and Calumet, owned by Mr. Emery, of Old Judge cigarrette fame. On the left is Grennell and Twin Island. The steamer stops at Thousand Island Park to take what is generally considered half the passengers which constitutes her load. Again, on our way we pass around the head of Wells Island, and have a view on the right of the finest avenue in the Park, a long line of boat-houses, and a number of steam yachts, sail and fishing boats, windmills, etc., etc. Beyond, on the right, is Hemlock Island and Hotel, owned by Mr. Garrison, of Syracuse. On the left is Grennell's Island and house, where the boat stops for passengers; beyond, on the right, is Otsego Point and cottages. We next pass two cottages, after which Picton Isle. Beyond is Eel Bay; on the left, beneath the brow of the hill, is where the American Canoe Club holds in annual convention. On Grindstone Island, which is in Jefferson County, N. Y., there are 500 inhabitants on the island, all Republicans. They, however, all voted the Democratic ticket Presidential year, which elected Cleveland. After leaving Grindstone Island we cross the boundary line between the United States and Canada, after which we arrive at many very pretty islands, on the right as well as on the left.

AMONG THE ISLANDS.

It must not be supposed that these hundreds of Islands are all occupied and have cottages on them, or laid out with walks and fountains. For every island that has a house on it there are perhaps twenty that have none. The number of houses are increasing every year, and I think that in time nearly every island will be occupied in the Canadian channel as they are in the American.

On the left is Darling's dock, the famous wood station. We have as yet never seeen the "Darling," although the dock is always visible. It may be she is busy in the pantry washing dishes.

GANANOQUE.

Here the captain announces a stay of twenty-five minutes for refreshments, remarking also that it takes twelve minutes to walk up town and twelve minutes back, with the remainder for refresh, which seems to my mind a little too fresh. Leaving Gananoque on time, we will return by the Canadian channel, which is more wild and picturesque, as far as scenery is concerned, although not one island or point is inhabited here to ten in the American channel.

On the right is Kipp Island. Passing many beautiful islands and lighthouse, we arrive at Halstead's Bay—after passing which the islands come thick and fast, all sizes and shapes, from a little one for a cent to those done up in bunches like asparagus, and you get a bunch for five. We soon arrive at Lind Light, on the right, and are coming to the Fiddler's Elbow: Lay this book aside at this point and feast the eye, for no one could do the subject of a description justice. We soon emerge from our land, or island-locked, channel, and approach Darling's dock. The dock is visible, but we have never seen the darling—after which comes Echo Point, where you can hear as many echoes as you pay cents fare. Passing a farm house on the right, we soon arrive on the left to Rockport; here you will observe we have but two seasons of the year, Ice and Rock; this is the rocky season. Turning to the right, we make direct for Westminster Park. Looking backward over the left shoulder, you will have a view of Idlewild and Sport Islands, owned by the Packers, of Pennsylvania. A better view of those islands may be obtained after leaving Westminster Park for Alexandria Bay. After passing the point, Hayden's Island, Fairyland comes in view. The little island, with cottage, is owned by Mr. Hasbrock, of Ogdensburg, N. Y., called Pike Island. The next on the right is St. John's Island, owned by Judge Donahue, of New York. The next on the right is Manhattan group, owned by Judge Spencer and Hasbrock, of New York. A wooden bridge joins them together. This is the first island inhabited for recreation, and was bought by Seth Green, the fish culturist of New York State; on the left is Long Beach,

Anthony's Point, Bonnie Castle, on the right is Dishler and Hart's Island. We next arrive at Alexandria Bay, from whence we started most four hours ago.

WHAT AND WHO MADE ALEXANDRIA BAY.

In 1872, President Grant visited this delightful spot, a guest of R. M. Pullman, of Palace car fame, Pullman Island. There was at that time inadequate hotel accommodations, for the tourist as well as the visitor who had been drawn to this the most beautiful natural scenery in the world. Messrs. Cornwall and Walton of Alexandria Bay, with their usual display of sense and sagacity, as well as business tact for which they have always been commended, offered to give the best site on the St. Lawrence to any man who would erect upon it, a first-class summer hotel. Mr. O. G. Staples, of Watertown, N. Y., hearing of this offer came, he saw, and how he conquered you shall know as we proceed with our narrative. Well, he concluded to father the scheme, securing a man with money, a Mr. Nott, of Syracuse, the ground, or rock rather, was broken January 14th, 1873, and the Thousand Island House was completed and opened July 17th, 1873, just six months from the day of starting. Rumor says that although their money gave out a little above the first story Staples' indomitable will saw it completed and furnished, ready to receive guests, just as soon and as well as if he had been a millionaire. During the next two years of the partnership of Staples and Nott, everything did not go as smooth as a marriage bell, but still they went, and in the end Staples had the money and hotel. (I hope the reader if he knows Staples will not be so unkind as to accuse him of parting with all his experience and make the pun that he took the money and Nott the experience.) Staples bought out Nott, and I believe, paid him what was agreed, and he run the hotel until April 15th, 1883, when Mr. R. H. Southgate, (the man of many hotels, too numerous to mention here), bought him out. The many changes that have been made, and those contemplated, and when completed, will make this the mecca of summer resort watering places, the Venice of America. I desire to say right here that I hope Mr. Southgate will not lose sight of what has in the past made the Bay popular as a resort. I like to see the standard of visitors raised as well as the prices. I would like it to be the place for fish as well as those who love the piscatorial art No dust, no dampness, no malaria or hay fever, no mosquitoes, light, dry air, cool and bracing. Thermometer never over 80 or below 50 in July and August, and one can enjoy what is denied them almost everywhere else, a good nine hours of cool refreshing sleep under a blanket. Those troubled with pulmonary complaints will find great relief here. Steamers, steam yachts and sailing vessels abound, everything to animate the scene and enhance the pleasure of visitors is done. Fishing, fishing boats, bathing, etc., as well as fish abounds, and we say here, if you have never been to the Bay come, if you have been come and see it under the new reign of Mr. Charles P. Clemes, and I know you will be pleased.

" YES ! A GREAS-Y STATUE."

" How much do you weigh ?" Well, I am asked that question many times every day, and as I am not sensitive will say my weight is three hundred and thirty pounds (in the shade). The reason why I say the shade is because there has never been raised a mathematician with the ability to compute the weight of a grease spot, and were I compelled to remain in the sun very long would make one, and do not care to mislead people into an error. The fat of this land is about as unequally distributed as the wealth. Those who ain't got it want it ; those who have it, have too much. I am therefore a Vanderbilt in grease—have a corner in lard, as it were.

"A LITTLE ONE ON PERKINS."

Two gentlemen at the Thousand Island House one day were talking, when the subject of truth was approached, and one of them who stammered, said, " There are t-t-three great li-liars i i-in America." The friend said, " Who are they ?" O-o-one of t-t-them i i-is T-T-Tom Oc-Oc-Ochiltree of Ta-Ta-Texas, and th-th-the other two is E-E-Eli Perkins.

VISITORS AT THE 1,000 ISLANDS,

who desire to vist Montreal and return by boat (their time being limited), the following information will be of interest. All passengers arrive in Montreal between six and seven o'clock p. m., as there is little to see at night and very little time to see it in. The boat leaves her dock, Canal Basin to return, every morning at 9 o'clock, except Sunday. You can remain in Montreal until the 12 M., train for Lachine from the G. T. R. Station, (by taking that train, fare 35 cents, you will arrive at Lachine in time to take the boat and enjoy your dinner while passing through Lake St. Louis.) Should you desire to prolong your stay, remain in Montreal until the 5

p. m. train leaves same depot for Coteau Landing. A carriage in waiting will take you to the boat, fare from Montreal, including carriage $1.25. You will take passage from there at seven o'clock, and have your supper on board of boat while passing through Lake St. Francis. As it takes the boat sixteen hours longer to come back, than to go down (reason they are compelled to pass through the Lachine, Bohomoise and Cornwall canals, which consumes the time). All passengers arrive at Alexandria Bay, every day, between one and two o'clock p. m., except on Monday.

WHAT I KNOW ABOUT CATCHING FISH.

During the summer of 1885 I was at the Thousand Island House, Alexandria Bay, N. Y., and took note of some of the best catches of fish, which with pleasure I give space here, that my friends may see, and those who may have heard that there is no good fishing at the Bay, a chance to judge. Let me first say that anybody can catch fish of the following varieties anywhere in the St. Lawrence River: Rock Bass, Black Bass, Perch, Pike, Pickerel and Muscalonge. I have caught, off the dock at the Bay, in less than two hours, a Black Bass weighing three and one half pounds and a Pickerel weighing over six pounds.

THE FISH CATCH OF 1885.

The fishing season commenced early and many prominent in the piscatorial art were early at the Bay and secured good catches. A party of gentlemen, among them being Mr. A. Ehrich of New York, caught, within a week, four Muscalonge weighing, respectively, 18, 21, 29 and 30 pounds. This catch was not beaten during the season, therefore Mr. Erich will receive the medal for the best catch of Muscalonge for the season of 1885.

Mr. B. E. Lockwood, Buckingham Lockwood, and his brother, of Norwalk, Conn., caught, June 27th, fifty Black Bass, eighteen weighing over 2 pounds each.

Mr. J. T. Easton, of New York, caught, June 28th, a Muscalonge weighing $20\tfrac{1}{2}$ pounds.

Mrs. E. A. Madden caught, July 6th, eleven Black Bass, one weighing three pounds ten ounces, and two over two pounds ; also two large Pickerel.

Mrs. W. A. Frazer caught fifty fish July 11th, 20 Black Bass, weighing from one to three pounds.

Little Julian Madden caught a Pickerel weighing three pounds off Thousand Island House dock.

Mr. L. G. Cairns, of Gainesville, Texas, caught thirteen Pickerel weighing from 3 to 8 pounds.

Miss Brown of New York, caught, in two hours, seven Black Bass and Pickerel weighing from $2\tfrac{1}{2}$ to 6 pounds.

Miss Jessie Schwardt, of New York, caught several Pickerel weighing from 7 to 10 pounds ; also a Black Bass $2\tfrac{1}{2}$ pounds.

Hon. R. B. Martine, District Attorney of New York, came home one evening after a day's sport bringing Black Bass over 2 pounds, some very large Pickerel and an Eel.

Mr. Bruce Price and wife, of New York, two experts at fishing, never came home without a very handsome catch. He is credited with catching the largest framed Black Bass ever seen at the Bay. Had he been as fat as the editor of this volume, would have weighed—well, you guess.

Mr. A. Wallack and wife of New York, caught several good catches of fish, but one day were not one quarter of a mile from the hotel, nor gone over two hours, and returned with ten Pickerel weighing from 3 to 8 pounds.

Mr. Robert G. McCord and wife, of New York, and party, caught, August 11th, twenty-three Black Bass weighing from 1 to 3 pounds. Mrs. McCord caught a Black Bass weighing nearly 4 pounds.

Mrs. Frazer and Mrs. Madden caught, August 7th, twenty-two Black Bass.

Mr. H. R. Clark, wife, and Mr. Post formed a party to go up the Reideau Canal in Canada as the spots for good sport at the Bay had become monotonous. They returned after eight days, and during a conversation with me said they would rather catch six one pound Black Bass at Alexandra Bay, with all its pleasant surroundings, than catch one hundred weighing 6 pounds each in any other waters on earth.

G. W. Morse, of Boston, Mass., caught a Pickerel weighing $10\frac{1}{2}$ pounds.

Hon. Judge Troy and wife, of Brooklyn, and party, caught in one day forty fish—Black Bass, Pike and Pickerel. The judge always takes his rifle along, and is sure to bring home some rare specimen of the feathered tribe to place in his collection at home. They say he is no amateur as a taxidermist.

Mr. J. A. Ehrich, of Ehrich Bros., New York, with a party of friends, on August 12th, caught one hundred and twenty-four Black Bass weighing from $1\frac{1}{2}$ to 4 pounds each.

Mr. A. Isaacs, wife, and Miss Cohen have never failed to bring in a good catch of Pickerel or Black Bass.

Judge Smith, R. G. McCord, C. M. Stone, Dr. W. C. Wheeler and party, of New York, August 15th, caught 325 Black Bass. Judge Smith caught the best or largest Black Bass (Oswego), $4\frac{1}{2}$ pounds.

Mr. William White and wife, Fort Plain, N. Y., Mr. J. Lowery and wife and Mr. Isaacs and friends formed a party August 17th. The catch included fifteen Pickerel weighing from 4 to 9 pounds and ten Black Bass weighing from 1 to 3 pounds.

Mr. Proctor and the Singer family caught ten Pickerel, the largest weighing $8\frac{1}{2}$ pounds, several Black Bass, and the largest Eel of the season.

Mr. George White, a fisherman, caught a Muscalonge, August 19th, weighing 10 pounds.

Mrs. L. H. Jauvrn and Miss Marie, of New York, caught two very large Pickerel and three Black Bass.

Mr. Philip Tillinghast, Mr. Julian Nathan and Mr. Charles J. Henry, of New York, caught, in sight of the Thousand Island House, what proved to be the largest Black Bass of the season. Mr. Tillinghast was the lucky one, and the fish weighed 4 pounds 2 ounces. Mr. Nathan came next with an Oswego Black Bass weighing $3\frac{1}{2}$ pounds. Mr. Tillinghast of the Miles Building, New York, takes the gold medal for the largest Black Bass caught for the season of 1885.

Mr. and Mrs. W. S. Neilson, of New York, caught in one day twenty-three Black Bass weighing from $1\frac{1}{4}$ to $3\frac{1}{2}$ pounds each.

F. G. Ringold and Mr. W. C. Compton, of Cincinnati, Ohio, who have been visitors at the Bay for the past thirty years, said to me last year that they were not troubled with the small shad this year as the year previous ; and the fishing must now improve since the restrictions were put upon nets, etc., by the Angler's Association.

Mr. H. R. Clark of New York, the most enthusiastic fisherman in these parts, has captured and destroyed in 1885 over ninety nets. Mr. Clark caught the largest fish ever landed with an 8-ounce rod on a single snell. The fish was a Sturgeon over 5 feet long, and weighed 78 pounds. He was one hour and five minutes landing him, which was great sport for Clark.

Mr. H. Merrell, of Montreal (firm of W. H. Merrell & Co.), caught at Hamilton's Island, 84 pounds of Pike and Pickerel, and four Bass weighing 4 lbs. each ; fourteen Pike weighed from 4 to 8 lbs. each. Mr. Merrell caught last season the largest Wall Eyed Pike ever taken from the St. Lawrence on an 8 oz. rod, $17\frac{1}{2}$ pounds weight. He is considered one of the best fishermen on the St. Lawrence.

Mr. Fulton, Mayor of Pittsburg, Mr. Higby, and a number of friends, with their wives, went fishing a number of times from the Bay last season. The number of fish captured, as well as the stories told by them, would fill a volume this size. I requested them to draw on Eli Perkins for facts, which will appear in the next edition of this work.

To those who say there is no fishing at Alexandria Bay (and do not want the earth), allow me to say Mr. H. R. Clark has a standing offer with me, to bet any man $10 that he can catch ten pounds of fish (any where within a mile of the Hotel) in an hour.

I am really sorry to cut this subject short, but space prevents my giving any more names and catches. The largest fish caught during the season was a Muscalonge, weighing 38 lbs., caught at an island opposite Rockport; the largest caught at the Bay, 18 lbs.; the largest Pike, $7\frac{1}{3}$ lbs.; the largest pickerel, 13 lbs., and the largest Bass, $5\frac{1}{2}$ lbs.   Respectfully yours,
                              E. F. BABBAGE.

"I OWE YOU AN APOLOGY,"

Dear reader, because since the first edition of this work it has claimed that there were no mosquitos at Alexandria Bay, but on at least three occasions when the wind was in a certain direction we were visited last year by at least a dozen or so. After a thorough search of three weeks, unable to find the cause, we were about to give it up when, to our astonishment, we discovered it. Upon looking up the hotel register we found that the hotel opened that year with twenty-seven guests, all from New Jersey. Comments are unneccessary. We found relief in attending Sunday School, and after the usual exercises were gone through with a collection was to be taken for the poor. The teacher, desiring to show the aptness of the pupils, asked each one as he put his mite into the box to recite an appropriate verse from the Bible. The first lad said, "The Lord loveth the cheerful giver," placed his mite in and took his seat. The second one said "He that giveth to the poor lendeth unto the Lord," and proudly took his seat. The third boy, more worldly than the rest, remarked "that a fool and his money soon parted."—He will sit down, if he can, at home.

A REAL LIVE DUDE

was at the Bay last season, and I must give him credit for one thing, if I could not for having either money or brains, but will say he was very attentive to the ladies, and it may be said to his credit he never tried to cut me out. One fine morning he induced three of the nicest young ladies at the Bay to take a boat ride, and for the privilege of their company agreed to do the rowing himself. They had been out upon the water for some time, and he had done the rowing heroically, but, getting into the strong current, his physical development was being tested to its utmost, when he asked the young ladies "if it would not be better for him to hug the shore." After a pause of a minute, the girliest girl of the group exclaimed: "Well, if you cannot find anything better to hug, do for heaven's sake, 'hug the shore!'"

SOME OF THE OWNERS.

St. John's five acres, Judge C. Donohue, New York.

Manhattan, five acres, Judge Spencer and J. L. Hasbrouck, New York.

Deshler, twelve acres, W. G. Deshler, Columbus, O.

Deer, twenty-five acres, S. Miller, Rochester, N. Y.

Fairy Land, twenty acres, C. H. and W. B. Hayden, Columbus, O.

Platt, two acres, Sisson & Fox, Alexandria Bay.

Brown's, ten acres, S. G. Pope, Alexandria Bay.

Pleasant, three acres, Sisson & Fox, Alexandria Bay.

Pullman's, three acres, George M. Pullman, Chicago, Ill.

Friendly, three acres, A. B. Parker and Abner Mellen, Jr., New York.

Cherry, eleven acres, A. B. Pullman and C. B. Marsh, of Chicago, Ill.; the Rev. George Rockwell, Fulton, N. Y.

Nobby, over three acres, H. R. Heath, New York.

Welcome, three acres, S. G. Pope, Ogdensburgh, N. Y.

Florence Proctor, one acre, E. R. Proctor, Cincinnati, O.

Maple, three acres, J. L. Hasbrouck, owner.

Netts, one-half acre, E. A. Kollymer, Brooklyn, N. Y.

Summer Land, ten acres, the Reverend Asa Saxe, D. D., Rochester, N. Y.; Almon Gunnison, D. D., Brooklyn, and Richmond Fisk, D. D., Syracuse, N. Y.

Isle Imperial, one acre, Mrs. LeCount, Philadelphia, Pa.

Linleth Gow, one-half acre, R. A. Livingston, New York.

Elephant Rock, one-fourth acre, T. C. Crittenden, Watertown, N. Y.

Idlewild, four acres, R. A. Packer, Sayre, Pa.

Arcadia and Ina, two acres, S. A. Briggs, New York.

Sport, four acres, H. A. Packer, Mauch Chunk, Pa.

Rye, J. H. Hunt, New York.

Kit Grafton, one-fourth acre, Mrs. S. L. George, Watertown, N. Y.

Island Mary, two acres, W. L. Palmer, Watertown, and James M. Browner, St. Louis.

Little Charm, one-eighth acre, Mrs. F. W. Barker, Alexandria Bay.

Frost, two acres, Mrs. Sarah L. Frost, Watertown.

Excelsior Group, five acres, C. S. Goodwin, Oneida, N. Y.

Resort, three acres, Pioneer Club, Watertown.

Island Royal, Royal E. Dean, New York.

Devil's Oven, one-fourth acre, has been fitted up with an observatory, H. R. Heath, New York.

Sylvan and Moss, three acres, S. T. Woolworth, Watertown, N. Y.

Cuba, five acres, W. F. Storey, Buffalo, N. Y.

Little Angell, one-eight acre, W. A. Angell, Chicago.

Little Lehigh, one acre, Col. R. B. Yates, Rochester, and C. H. Cummings, New York.

Warner's four acres.

Island Home, one acre, S. D. Hungerford, Adams, N. Y.

Sunny Side, one acre, Mrs. Emily Moak, Watertown, N. Y.

Wild Rose, one acre, W. G. Rose, Cleveland, Ohio.

No name, one-quarter acre, Mrs. F. Hammerkin, Syracuse, N. Y.

Harmony, one-quarter acre, Mrs. Celia Berger, Syracuse, N. Y.

Wynnstay, one acre, Mrs. Bergin, of Spuyten-Duyvel, N. Y.

Alice Isle, two acres, J. G. Hill, Brooklyn, N. Y.

Island Royal, Royal E. Deane (firm of Bramall, Deane & Co.), New York.

Sunbeam Group, one acre, C. E. Alling, Rochester, N. Y.

Walton, now Lotus Land, twenty-two acres, Mrs. J. N. Robins and Mrs. G. H. Robinson, of New York, purchased in 1883, will be improved by all the art at their command.

Bula Vista, Lodge Keepler Point, owned by Mr. Bosworth, of Milwaukee, Wis.

Seven Sister Isles, owned by Dr. Winston, of Washington, D. C.

Comfort, formerly Pratt and Centennial, owned by A. E. Clark, of Chicago Produce Exchange, who has spent $20,000 upon the spot to beautify it.

Deer Island, owned by Hon. Sam. Miller, of New Haven, Conn., formerly of Rochester, N. Y.

Melrose Lodge and Ingle Side, owned by Messrs. A. B. Pullman and C. B. Marsh.

Florence Island, owned by H. S. Chandler, of the Independent.

Two-Islands-in-Eel-Bay, two acres, E. L. Sargent, Watertown, N. Y.

Long Branch, ten acres, Mrs. C. E. Clark, Watertown, N. Y.

Nigger, three acres, Eugene Robinson, of New York.

Ella, one-quarter acre, R. E. Hungerford, Watertown, N. Y.

Lookout, two acres, Thomas H. Borden, New York.

Grinnell Island, two acres, D. G. Grinnell, Brooklyn, N. Y.

Douglass, three acres, Douglass Miller, New Haven, Conn.

Hub, opposite Alexandria Bay, owned by H. R. Clark's youngest son, a birthday present from Cornwall and Walton.

Hart's, five acres, E. Kirke Hart, Albion, N. Y.

Sunny-Side, two acres, Wm. Stickenson, Sayre, Pa.

Wau Winnett, two acres, Mr. Hill, Chicago, Ill.

WESTMINSTER PARK.

Opposite the Thousand Island House, is Westminster Park, on the lower end of Wells Island. It is eight miles long and from three to four miles wide. On the other side of it is the Canadian channel of the river, about half a mile wide. The lower end of the Island is separated into two parts by one of the prettiest sheets of water that ever rippled against the bows of a canoe. This is called the "Lake of the Island," and it is connected with the river, on both the American and Canadian sides, by a narrow channel. The Lake is five or six miles long, as smooth as glass, and is altogether too pretty and too romantic to attempt to describe.

Westminster Park was bought in 1874 by a Presbyterian stock company, and it now has about 15 miles of drives and some fine buildings. It has two long water fronts—one on the American side of the river, and the other on the Lake of the Island, on the Canadian side, there is a high hill on the island called Mount Beulah, though after climbing it I think the Hill Difficuity would be a more appropriate name. There is a large chapel on the top of the hill, known as Bethune Chapel, with seating accomodations for a thousand persons, and with a tower 136 feet high, (was blown down in March, 1885,) affording a beautiful view of the river and the islands The name of the chapel recalls the fact that the late Rev. Dr. Geo. W. Bethune was the pioneer tourist through this region, and until his death continued to come here summer after summer for recreation.

BONNIE CASTLE.

"Timothy Titcomb" (Dr. J. G. Holland, editor of Scribner's Monthly), chose this point as a haven of rest and recuperation, and who does not commend his choice. It will be remembered that he died in New York shortly after leaving his cherished Bonnie Castle in 1881, for his ardous winter's labors. Light house in the distance.

A LETTER FROM SETH GREEN.

NEW YORK STATE FISHERY COMMISSION.

Office of the Superintendent.

ROCHESTER, N. Y., March 20th.

MY DEAR LITTLE "PHAT BOY":

You request of me a letter for your book. Letter writing is not my forte, but you are welcome to use these facts. In 1855 I bought an island and named it Manhattan, near Alexandria Bay, built house upon it in the fall and moved there with my family the next spring and lived there during the summers of 1856 and 1857. The year of 1858 I spent a part of the season with a party of prominent gentlemen. During the time I was there, if I wanted black bass for breakfast I could take my two fly rods and take from 5 to 10 black bass by trolling around my island of 4 acres, and at any time after August 1st, I could take my gun and kill a mess of ducks in a short time. There was a few deer on Welles Island then. I have killed 50 ducks in one day among the islands, and I could take 100 black bass with fly any day I wished.

Immediately opposite is Hart's Island, back of which is Deshler. Next on the left is

MANHATTAN,

the first island on which habitation was attempted. It was bought by Mr. Seth Green, the fish culturist of N. Y., in 1855. He built a cottage upon it and for several years spent his summers here. Mr. J. L. Hasbrouck and Judge

J. C. Spencer, of N. Y., purchased it from him. They have spent $15,000 upon the Island. The original cottage built by Seth Green still remains and is used by them as a dining room.

Between Deshler and Manhattan, looking backward, is Fairyland, owned by C. H. and W. B. Hayden, of Columbus, Ohio. This is really one of the finest islands in the river. At a vast expense art has triumphed over nature, transforming a barren into the loveliest of green lawns. Next on the left is deer island; then

SUMMERLAND.

Summerland, one of the most beautiful of the "Thousand Islands," is located mid-way between the north and south channels of the St. Lawrence, about three miles below Alexandria Bay, having an area of fourteen acres and is the largest of the "Summerland group," which includes "Idlewild," "Sport," "Ida" and "Arcadia." The island is covered with a dense forest furnishing an abundance of shade and is said to have the finest groves on the river. At the extreme northerly and southerly ends of the island there are extensive sandy beaches, a great rarity in this locality, which are used by the "Summerlanders" for bathing purposes. The island is traversed from end to end by a most delightful natural avenue, densely shaded and lined on either side with a thick undergrowth of wild flowers and ferns. The island is owned by the Summerland Association, a corporation organized under and by virtue of the laws of the State of New York, for social and yachting purposes, and composed of the following stockholders: Rev. Asa Saxe, D. D., Isaiah F. Force, James Sargent,

Sears E. Brace, Emory B. Chase, Henry C. Wisner, Lewis P. Ross, Francis M. McFarlin, Chas. W. Gray, George H. Newell, Henry O. Hall, Joseph A. Stull and Frank W. Hawley, of Rochester, N. Y. ; Rev. Richmond Fish, D. D., Alfred Underhill and Horace Bronson of Syracuse, N. Y. ; Rev. Almond Gunnison, D. D., and Frank Sperry, of Brooklyn, N. Y, The association have erected upon the island a large and commodious " Club House," wherein the members of the association and their families take their meals.

After setting apart a large grove at each end of the island for general use, the balance of the island was divided into lots, one of which was assigned to each stockholder. Upon these lots so assigned, the members of the association have erected cottages for the sole use of their own families.

In addition to the Club House the association has erected numerous pavilions and summer houses in different parts of the island, together with a large ice house, and has constructed several docks of sufficient size to permit of the landing of large steamers.

The association owns a large steam yacht, which is used in running to and from Alexandria Bay and for fishing and pleasure excursions.

Each member of the association provides himself with sailing and row boats. The Club House is opened for the reception of the members of the association and their immediate families *only*, on the first day of July of each year, and remains open until about September 15th, during all of which time the yacht is at the service of the party.

Between Deer Island and Summerland is Cedar; back of Cedar is Sport, owned by H. A. Packer, who died in 1884. The island, however, will be occupied this year by H. C. Wilbur, G. B. Linderman, C. B. Newton and other friends. Anthony Point is on the right. This place is the resort of E. and T. H. Anthony, the extensive dealers in photographic goods in New York.

APING CUSTOMS, MANNERS, ETC., OF THE ENGLISH.

This is done to a great extent, not only in Canada, but I am sorry to say in Free America, better known as the U. S. I cannot find any fault with the average Canadian, who is, as it were, governed by Queen Victoria, and must have some reverence for royalty in the aping of their manners and customs, but in this land where we have an abundance of Queens, Princes, Lords and Sovereigns who are not flattered by titles, but bear their honors meekly, all are royal born and bred. Speaking of titles reminds me that at home I am plain Edward F. Babbage, or "Phat Boy," (I spell it with 'Ph' because it does not sound so greasy), but the moment I leave home, say for a trip through the South, I am called Captain for the first few hundred miles, then a little way on its becomes Colonel, and when I get to Georgia it is Major, in South Carolina it is Judge or General, until I get to Florida, and I have heard them say there "great God is that you ?" But we diverge. Returning to the aping of the manners of Princess Louise, I wish to say right here that I firmly believe it did the Canadian people a great amount of good, but fail to see where the people of the United States could be benefitted. I was told that at Kingston the Princess asked for her strawberries in a box with hulls on, and when placed before her she took them up by the stem between the thumb and finger and bit the berry off and placed the hull on the plate. Now everybody does the same; previous to her visit they used to hull and wash them before placing them on the table. The same with grapes. They used to wash them in a goblet of water at the table before eating them; now they take the grape between the thumb and finger, press it to the lips and squeeze gently, and juice as well as insides are soon on the way to digestion, and the skin laid away on the plate as the Princess did. Asparagus—it was almost painful for me to see Canadians eat it in as many ways as there were people at the table, in fact no two ate it alike until after the Princess came; now everybody takes it by the hard green end, between thumb and finger, and putting it into the mouth, closes the teeth down upon it and draws it gently from the mouth, leaving all that is digestible within, and the remainder is laid on the plate. The Princess once took a walk through her kitchen at Rideau Hall, Ottawa, took the vegetable cook to task for washing fresh picked peas from the vine that had just been shelled, saying it was nonsense, if your hands are clean, to wash a virgin pea.

HOW WOMEN FISH.

Having read various descriptions of how fishing is carried on by the fair sex at the several watering places, permit us to mention some of them. One writer said: "Ah! what joy to have a bite; what rare delight to find one's bait gone"—and it was only by the suicidal policy of some water-weary fish who chance to pass our way that we could record one fish for our day's sport. How different is the fishing at the Bay. I have known Mrs. A. Isaacs and daughter, of Brooklyn, to catch in four hours 20 fish, two of which weighed over 25 pounds. A gentleman says of the fishing near the Hudson: "The first thing a woman d es when she goes fishing is to make herself look as hideous as possible—a sort of a cross between the Witch of Endor and Meg Merrilles. This is done by a hideous straw hat big enough to cover a chicken coop, the oldest and most unbecoming dress she has got, a pair of gloves six sizes too large, and, if possible rubber boots ; and the sight of woman, lovely woman, so dressed presents a spectacle of pity." You will not have occasion to pity any of the ladies who go fishing from the Bay, for they look so jaunty you would envy them and their enjoyment as well as fish. I have known Mrs. Madden and party to bring home 30 fish, from a 3¼ black bass to a 7 ℔ pickerel. A friend writes from C—— Lake, telling how he spent a day fishing there, accompanied by three ladies and a gentleman friend. Women never step into a boat here, but always jump. Of course she slips, falls down, yells for help, nearly upsets the boat, and is put to rights by the most eligible young man in the party. Nothing will do, then, but she must row, and she knows as much about rowing as a cow does about billiards. She handles her oars as if they were trees, splashes every one with water, blisters her hands, and after half an hour's work she is about ten feet away in the wrong direction, when one of the men takes the oars and we are soon at our fishing place. She tries to bait her hook, and after getting the hook into all her fingers, in fact everywhere but into the minnow, her friend baits the hook, and she throws it out. The first time it catches on to one of the ladies' ears, the next throw, into the back of the gentleman's neck, and the third time into the coat of her friend, who quietly cuts it out (it is his best coat), and he quietly puts the line into the water without saying a cuss word, and says he hopes she will catch a whale. After a few moments of quiet all are informed she has a bite; she pulls it in steadily, to find it is part of the carcass of a dead horse. She is soon relieved of the burden and catches a small perch. She is so delighted that she must let it flop into the faces of every one in the boat, tries for twenty minutes to take it off the hook, but her fingers are so sore she lets the job out to her male companion. One of the other ladies has sat for two hours without moving a muscle, while the other, I believe, would fish with a hair-pin baited with a piece of red flannel hung to a skein of silk in a stationary wash tub, and swear solemnly when she got through that she had millions of bites. Dear lady readers, we have no such experiences to relate at Alexandria Bay. The boats are the prettiest, the fishermen the nicest, the fish the largest and best, the boatmen bait your hooks; the hotel furnishes the lunch, and you are sure to catch fish; and when they are cooked and you eat your meal served upon an Island, and do not say you have had the most pleasant day ever spent fishing, draw on me for the balance. P. B.

YACHTING.

Water—and as one enthusiastic writer puts it—such water!—is abundant, and to enjoy this water in a pensive or poetic mood, the steam yacht should be brought into

requisition. Private yachts are numerous and elegant, and
it is to the credit of the owners that they are not niggardly
in exhibiting a spirit of generosity and courtesy. They are
constantly inviting individuals and parties to enjoy the
exhilerating excitement of the shooting around the beautiful spots. And if you, dear tourist, have no friend that
invites you to share a cushioned seat in his graceful fairy
like craft, then go to Capt. E. W. Visger, on the *Island
Wanderer*, or Capt. Sweet, of the *John Thorn*, and they
will take you on an excursion among the Islands that you
will gladly recall as a cheerful reminiscence of your St.
Lawrence excursion, for the opportunity will have been
offered to bring within the range of your vision enchanting
scenes that pen is not adequate to describe, but by purchasing one of the " Phat Boy's " Birds-eye Charts of the
St. Lawrence, you will be the possessor of the only correct
map of the St. Lawrence. A perfect guide to the river.

Still continuing our course, looking to the right, is the
cottage of Mrs. Clark, of Watertown. Next, Goose Bay is
the island owned by Dr. Carleton, near which is the Three
Sisters' Island; before the Three Sisters' is Hume's Island.
Next, on the left, is Whiskey Island, and on the right opposite are a number of large and small islands, the names of
which we will not weary the tourist's brain with.

Goose Bay is really beautiful, if its name is slightly
homely. It is studded with islands, and fishing abounds.
It is here that Mr. Hurbert R. Clark, of New York, in one
day caught some 300 pounds of black bass, ranging in
weight from $1\frac{1}{2}$ pounds to $6\frac{1}{2}$ pounds. On the right is
Lyon's dock and Meeker's island. Next, on the left, is

Three Sisters light; in the distance is Lone Star, or Dark Island; Island No. 1, it is called by some. After passing, on the left is a small cluster of island shoals. On the right is Chippewa Bay. This is a superb sheet of water, where the fishing is a marked feature. It is a favorite resort of Ogdensburg people, who occupy the contiguous islands. All around the shore are camps, cottages, etc., and make an animated scene for the tourist. Three miles from Chippewa Bay on the left is Crossover light; thence three miles to Cole's light on the left, where we enter the Canadian channel. Nine miles in the distance is Brockville. On the right opposite Cole's light is Oak point. Four miles below is Allen's landing, a very popular place for picnics, etc. On the left a prominent bluff. On the right for six miles the islands come thick and fast; huge rocks rise from the water's surface, with very little vegetation or foliage, and the boat makes her way rapidly among them, winding around like a snake, heading for all the points of the compass, frequently getting herself into coves and bays that apparently have no outlet, but always finding a channel, and sailing triumphantly out into the broad waters again.

A little beyond is St. Lawrence Park, used for pleasure and picnic parties, especially by our Canadian friends of Brockville. We are now at the village of Brockville; we "take a rest" for route B.

In front of Brockville are the last three of the Thousand Islands; being some distance from the rest, it is presumable they drifted away, and finally rooted here. This, however, was "long befo' the wah!"

Opposite, on the right, is Morristown, a small, lively American village, of about 1,000 inhabitants, a station on the Utica and Black River R. R., connects with Brockville by two steam ferries.

This is a picture of my twin brother, Dr. E. F. BABBAGE, of Rochester, N. Y. "A friend in need." How I wish I was a doctor.

"PHAT BOY."

ROUTE B.

Our object being to make this little book a complete Guide to the Thousand Islands and St. Lawrence River, so that tourists from any section, no matter where they strike, will find it intelligible to learn their location. We have therefore divided the explanation into two routes. First, we took our friends from New York to Niagara Falls, Lewiston, Toronto, Kingston and the American channel of the St. Lawrence as far as Brockville. Second, our journey will be from Cape Vincent, thence down the St. Lawrence through the American channel to Brockville.

CAPE VINCENT

is a pleasant little village in Jefferson county, N. Y., at the junction of Lake Ontario and the St. Lawrence River. It is also the terminus of the Rome, Watertown and Ogdensburg Railroad, and connections by steamer St. Lawrence are made to Alexandria Bay.

As we steam out of this port, on the left is Long, or Wolf Island, 21 miles in length and 7 miles in width. The next on the right is

CARLETON ISLAND.

At the upper extremity, the land narrows into a rugged promontory, ending in a bluff sixty feet in height. Here, lifting their ruined heads aloft, and plainly visible to all passers along the river, stand a number of toppling and half ruined chimneys. These may be seen for miles around. So long have these old sentinels watched over the scenes around them that their history is lost in the misty past. Around them are the remaining ruins of an old fort, supposed by many to be the ruins of old Fort Frontenac. Around its old redoubts and parapets linger antiquated historical legends and traditions enough to fill a volume, and forming an interesting study. An ancient well, cut in the solid Trenton limestone down to the level of the lake, has been converted by the reckless imaginations of the natives into a receptacle of the golden doubloons which the French soldiers, upon evacuating the old fort, are said to have thrown there, with the brass guns on top of them. Upon either side, and immediately in front of the bluff upon which the old fort stands, is a quiet, pretty little bay, which may once have supplied a safe and easy anchorage for the vessels that lay under its protecting guns.

The fortress is supposed to have been one of importance as a military post at some time, having been built upon an excellent plan and in the most substantial manner. Numbers of graves still occupy a field near by, the remains of the brave soldiers who once occupied the fort. The scene is of deep interest to the students of history.

About six miles this side of Clayton is Lindsay Island, the only one on the right between Cape Vincent and Clayton. On the left, two miles before reaching Clayton, is Grindstone Island, five miles long. Cross-over channel is where the Canadian line of steamers, leaving Kingston at 5 o'clock in the morning, comes through into the American channel. Before landing at Clayton is Prospect Park and hill, which has been systematically laid out for villas and camping parties, and where tourists can always find a comfortable stopping place. Although we have been traveling among the islands quite early in the morning, we have noticed that the people who occupy the cottages are all up, the ladies sitting on the piazzas reading, generally, and the gentlemen out in small boats fishing. There are two kinds of fishing done here—fishing for fun and fishing for fish. I cannot explain the distinction better than to repeat what a gentleman who was traveling with the party, said to me one afternoon: "We are going to take the ladies out fishing to-morrow," he said, "to give them a taste of the sport. Then, the next day, we are going out alone to catch some fish."

"DON'T DO IT."

This startling head-line, when it strikes the eye, denotes that there is something to be said of personal benefit to the reader of the article, and we hope to make it pleasant as well as profitable to those who take the time to peruse it. To begin with, we desire to say, don't get fat; do not allow yourself to develop beyond the line which is laid down for the average man or woman: because, if you do, the average chair will not fit, the average seat in a railroad coach will be too small; you will be obliged to shrink into it, and then take up the seat of another after you get in. The same trouble will occur at amusements, which you enjoy very much, but it so distorts you to occupy the chair that the pleasure is lost; the average door to a hack is too small, and so is the omnibus, and you are obliged to walk. Here you will enjoy it, especially if it is a little slippery, dropping now and then three hundred and thirty pounds, because your friend thinks it does not hurt a fat man to fall. You will get no sympathy from any one; this I will guarantee, because I have tried it. By way of illustration, if I had not eaten anything for three days but a yard of pump water, and was to come to a friend and say I was hungry, and had not had anything to eat for three days, he would look me all over, and in reply would say: "Well, I guess you can stand it until next fall." So the fleshier you are the least spmpathy you get; and if Dr. Tanner stood it for forty days, you have sufficient fat to last you six months, to say the least. Second, you become, as it were, a curiosity, and all look at you with amazement and wonder what circus or side show you escaped from, or to what dime museum you belong. Third, there isn't anything made for the average man that will fit you, therefore, everything must be made to order that you wear, except a necktie, pair of socks or handkerchief. The latter must be seven-eighths of a yard wide in order to hold the perspiration it will mop up in once passing over your manly brow. Fourth, when at the age of 21, and weighing 225 pounds, I had no trouble in making a selection of a partner for life. She climbed the golden stairs about five years ago, and now I am fair, fat, funny and forty; would pass in a crowd for 39, if my daughter was not around. If I find one now who loves a fat man—I am a little too fat—therefore, this world is a very chilly one for me.

After you become a little above the average size, as I have in development and are conspicuous, everybody will know you; if they do not, it will be easy for them to find out; all they are obliged to do is to ask anyone. You will not know only those of your relations and friends very near to you. Then this world will be very lonesome and cold, or your experience will be different from mine. It would be a treat (were you not sensitive) if you could walk one block and hear the expressions that come from the vulgar throng as they pass. One female, with eyes like two saucers, exclaimed: " Glory be to the father, Mary Ann, phwat's that?" And another say "Got in himmell, what a fat man," or a lady of color declare, " Umph! Umph!! Dat am de biggest man I ebber seed."

FROM BROCKVILLE TO MONTREAL.

Brockville was named in honor of General Brock, who fell in the Battle of Queenstown Heights in 1812. It is situated on the Canadian side of the St. Lawrence River, and is one of the pleasantest villages in the province It lies at the foot of the Thousand Islands on an elevation of land which rises from the river in a succession of ridges. The town was laid out in 1802, and is now a place of considerable importance. The present population is about 7,000.

After leaving the wharf, the boat passes the most beautiful cliff on the river, the Palisades of the St. Lawrence, on which are erected magnificent mansions and suburban residences and villas of Canada's distinguished sons. The most prominent of these is the son of Sir Hugh Allen, whose residence is really superb. The sightseer can observe the winding stairs, boat and bath houses and other appointments for recreation.

Having left Brockville, a magnificent view greets the eye; islands are not now in view; the river is a most beautiful sheet of water, running perfectly straight for about sixteen miles with the land on either side in good view, for the river is a little over two miles wide. Three miles from Morristown, on the right, is a camp ground of the Baptist persuasion, mostly from St. Lawrence County. Five miles on the left from Brockville is Maitland. At this point is a prominent object known as the old distillery, whose proprietor is said to have been worth, at one time, a million dollars, but whose cupidity during "America's unpleasantness" led him into selling " crooked whiskey," or rather disposing of his distillery products in a very " crooked way." Without giving the details, the facts in brief are: He antagonized the Canadian government in the matter of paying revenue, and in his fight for stupid supremacy, he not only lost his distillery, but his fortune too, and he and his family became reduced to poverty, and none of them remain around their former home. It is said he first induced his niece to marry the revenue collector of the district, that he might carry on the nefarious business in collusion and without detection, but, you see,

" The deep laid plans of mice and men gang aft aglee."

About four miles below, on the left, is the old blue stone church in the graveyard of which rests the remains of the founder of Methodism on this continent, Barbara Heck. One mile farther, on the left is McCarthy's new brick brewery. Half a mile beyond is the celebrated Rysdick stock farm, owned by J. P. Wiser, M. P. Here is owned the celebrated stallion Rysdick, which cost Mr. Wiser $25,000. It is a farm of about six hundred acres, and is unquestionably the finest stock farm in the Dominion of Canada. The thrift, energy and ability of this gentleman will not be wondered at when it is learned that he is of American birth. Next, on the left, is the celebrated Labatt's brewery and

PRESCOTT.

with its 3,000 inhabitants, who seem to have lost their grip on the trade of the river, judging from the dilapidated condition of the stores, warehouses. etc., on the wharves. The town, however, is handsomely laid out, has a fine city hall and market, and there are many fine private residences. It is connected with Ottawa, capital of the Dominion, by the St. Lawrence and Ottowa Railroad, distance 54 miles. Here many tourists who desire to visit the capital disembark for that purpose. We refer the tourist to Daniel's Hotel as a good stopping place. L. H. Daniels has taken the hotel, and spent $8,000 in improvements; he is too well known to the traveling public to need any praise from me. Opposite is

OGDENSBURG,

founded by Francis Picquit in May, 1749. It now contains about 10,000 people, and of course ranks as a city. It is the terminus of the Rome and Watertown, Utica and Black River, and the Ogdensburg and Lake Champlain railroads.

It is beautifully laid out, well planted with maple trees, and is called the " Maple City." It has a United States Custom House, post-office, and a new opera house, costing $150,000, six fine church edifices, water works, gas works, a fire alarm telegraph and two daily newspapers, and possibly other modern improvements. At the lower end of town is the big elevator of the Ogdensburg and Lake Champlain Railroad.

One mile and a half below Prescott, on the left, is Windmill point; the old windmill has been turned into a lighthouse. Here, in 1837, the "Patriots," under Von Shultz a Polish exile, established themselves, but from which they were driven with severe loss. We believe this Von Shultz was subsequently hung by the Canadian authorities, and his followers banished, probably to New Jersey. On the left, a little below the light-house, is the residence and farm of W. H. McGannon, the oldest pilot on the St. Lawrence river, the man who first took the Passport of the Richelieu line down the Long Sault Rapids, in July, 1847. I am also indebted to him for the correctness of my New Map of the St. Lawrence and other information of benefit to me and the public.

Three miles below, on the left, is Johnstown Bay, with Johnstown—not a very important trading post—overlooking. This place has a custom house officer, commissioner of fisheries, mayor and marshal of the district; but these important officials are concentrated in one man.

We turn here to the right, leaving the far-famed Chimney Island on the left, on which are said to be the ruins of old French forts, battlements, etc. The only remains we have discovered of these supposed formidable defences is an ex-

tensive moat around the island, twelve feet deep, filled with water. The chimney, from which it derives its name, is supposed to be on the island, but we have looked in vain to discover it. It may be, however, that it has floated down the river; we will speak of it further on.

In the distance, on the left, are Tick, or Pier islands. Some of the finest bass fishing in the river is off this old pier. Dr. Melville, of Prescott, the inventor of rheumatic victor, and an enthusiastic fisherman of this section, last summer caught a black bass weighing seven and one-half pounds while enjoying the sport around the pier.

Three miles from Chimney island in the distance, is what is termed "the cut," forming the channel between Galop and Moore's islands. It was the former channel of this line of boats, but the Dominion government are expending six millions of dollars for the enlargement of the canals of this route, and the survey party at present are blasting a channel through the

GALOP RAPID,

which may be seen in the distance. The reason of the change of channel is formed with an edict of the pilots not to interfere with the work of the engineer corps engaged on this necessary improvement of excavating a fifteen foot channel, to allow larger boats to pass, and dispense with the use of the Edwardsburg canal. This is the first and smallest rapid on the St Lawrence River, and as the Phat Boy has termed it, "a little one for a cent." I will, however, give you an idea of what the rapids are. All the rapids on this river are caused by numerous rocks, large and small, in the bed of the river, and the swift current of water passing over these rocks causes the fearful commotion that you observe. Now, to carry our philosophy a little farther, we say the larger the rock and the stronger the current, the better the rapids. No rocks, no water, no current, no rapids! This commotion which you see here is caused by a ledge of rocks five and one-half feet in height under nine feet of water. You can see the swell and white cap which this rock occasions, and then use your best judgment to determine the height of the rocks in Long Sault, where we hope to arrive at one o'clock. (There are, let me state here, eight rapids on our trip to-day, which may be divided into two classes, first and second. The first class are Long Sault, meaning a long leap or jump; Cedar, deriving its name from the trees in the vicinity, and Lachine. The second class are Galop, meaning a hopping, jumping rapid; Rapid Platt, meaning in French, flat; Chateau du Lac, meaning foot of the lake; Split Rock, derived from a fissure which makes the channel, and the Cascade, from its resemblance to a cascade).

On the left, before arriving at the Galop rapids, is the entrance to the Edwardsburg canal. This canal is seven and one-half miles in length, and is the first canal we arrive at; its terminus is at Iroquois. It would be well here to say that we only have canals around the rapids, or where the current is too strong for a steamer to ascend. We here append a tabular statement of the

ST. LAWRENCE CANALS.

Edwardsburg canal, $7\frac{1}{2}$ miles long, three locks, 14 feet fall in the river; Morrisburg canal, 4 miles long, 2 locks, 11 1-6 feet fall; Farron's Point canal, $\frac{3}{4}$ mile long, 1 lock,

4 feet fall; Cornwall canal, 12 miles long, 7 locks, 48 feet fall; Beauharnor's canal, 11½ miles long, 9 locks, 84 feet fall; Lachine canal, 9 miles long, 5 locks, 45 feet fall.

In the distance, on the left is the village of Edwardsburg, now called Cardinal. Here is located the Edwardsburg starch factory, the largest in the Dominion of Canada. The president of the company is the Hon. Walter Shanley, of Hoosac Tunnel fame. He was the great contractor who completed that wonderful piece of work, and is now manager of the St. Lawrence and Ottawa Railroad.

Twenty minutes from Edwardsburg to the next point of interest.

WHAT I KNOW ABOUT ELI PERKINS.

Some few years ago, Mr. Perkins was a passenger on one of the boats. I do not know whether he took me for the captain, director or manager of the line or not, but he exerted himself considerably to form my acquaintance. There was nothing unusual about that, however, as there is something "*distingue*" about me, and when on the boat I stand considerably "above proof." I have frequently dined at the same table with the Governor-General, Lord Dufferin and retinue—after his lordship had left. But to return to Eli. The day in question I was upon the deck of the boat as usual, describing the points of interest, especially the one on the Canadian shore, where the St. Regis Indians come year after year to gather the famous elm and basswood with which to make their celebrated baskets. I was delineating at some length upon the noble red man, when Eli came to me and said, I will write you a verse of poetry about that.

Glad to get a memento in that shape from so distinguished an individual, who had so often been accused of being witty, I said it would please me very much. Here is the verse:

> " Once here the noble red man took his delights,
> Fit, fished and bled ;
> Now most of the inhabitants are white,
> With nary a red."

I thanked him very profusely, and on subsequent occasions took great delight in repeating the lines to the passengers—never forgetting for a moment to remind them that they were written for me by the alleged American humorist. One day, after delivering myself of the poetry and repeating to the passengers that it was written by the celebrated poet, writer, humorist and lecturer, Eli Perkins, I was approached by an exceedingly polite and affable gentleman, whom I learned was Mr. John H. Rochester, of Rochester, N. Y., who asked if he understood me correctly in attributing the authorship of the lines quoted to Mr. Perkins. I assured him that he had written them expressly for me, and produced in Eli's own handwriting the original copy. With a subdued smile resting upon his countenance, Mr. Rochester informed me that there must be an error somewhere, as a gentleman, a Mr. Fletcher had written a poem in 1834, in which the exact verse occurred, and he proceeded to repeat the verse from memory. This took me slightly back, and I subsequently came to the conclusion with "my friend" of the *Oil City Derrick*, that a cabbage leaf was never more at home than when in the crown of " Uli Perkins' hat." After that I had no more use for the poem, but determined if I ever met "Uli" I should call to his mind the circumstances connected with " his little poem." I had not long to wait, for one day, while in Evansville, Indiana, at the St. George Hotel, I met the gentleman, and recalled the circumstance connected with the little verse, and he, with a perfect air of *nonchalance*, said that he had never given it a thought since—dashed it off in a minute. I told him how remarkable it was that great minds often run in the same channel, and related my experience with his gem. He scowled, and, turning on his heel, said it was indeed a singular word for word resemblance, but changed the subject at once, and asked me to his room on the following morning, which invitation I cheerfully accepted, doting all the evening upon having a nice time, and swopping a few gags, etc., etc.; but my hopes were blighted, for the next morning I was informed of his very early departure—gone up to lie to the people of Rockport, I was told. "Uli" is a great man, and contracts a larger amount of business upon a very small amount of capital than any public character I know of. When Eli reads this I expect he will load his big gun—not intellectual, but otherwise—and come for me. I will, therefore, give him a pointer in advance; there won't anything scare me but a stomach pump.

Distinguished among Indian names is that of Iroquois. Here it names a village, formerly known as Matilda; but, like all other good Matildas do, she changed her name to Iroquois, in order to preserve the name. The Iroquois Indians formerly owned this section of country. One and a half miles below this village is the narrowest point in the St. Lawrence River, from Kingston to the gulf. This broad expanse of water we are just passing, and the one we arrive at immediately after leaving the point, are very shallow, consequently holds the water in check at the point—the depth of water in the shallow places being about 22 feet, while at the point it is 84 feet. Width of the river 1,140 feet—170 feet less than a quarter of a mile.

On the right in the narrowest portion of the river is Cedar Point. On the left is a small bluff, formerly called Hemlock Point, on account of a fine hemlock standing there; but on one fine morning the hemlock, the tree and the point all slid into the river, and have not yet returned. About fifteen feet back from the point is a rail fence, which is outside of the earth-works that were thrown up in 1812–13, and batteries were erected on Cedar Point.

On the left is the main shore of the Dominion of Canada, with a population of over five millions. On the right is the main shore of the United States of America, with a population of over fifty millions. When the five millions want those fifty millions all they will be obliged to do is to walk over and take them. Then will be verified that beautiful passage in Holy Writ which says, "One shall chase a thousand and two put ten thousand to flight. Sing!"

This was really a strong point, and was fortified on both sides of the river by the opposing parties. From the fact of the successful fortifications by the Americans the Rideau Canal owes its origin. Guns and stores or merchandise could not be taken up the river. It was conceived by Colonel By, of the Engineer corps, that a new canal would obviate the difficulty, and all his resources were immediately put into requisition, and the canal was completed at a cost of $5,000,000. It extends from Ottawa, formerly By-town, to Kingston, and is still in use.

Ten minutes from here to the next point of interest. On the left is the entrance to the Morrisburg Canal, the second canal in the chain, but it is not used by this linè of boats. All tows and sailing vessels have to use the canal. In the distance front is Rapid Platt; on the right is Ogden's Island, the finest wooded island in the St. Lawrence River. Beyond is Waddington, St. Lawrence county, N. Y. In front is this rapid we have just named; it is the second one, and is a "little one for two cents." It has, however, eight feet more descent than the first, but is only a one cent *descenter* rapid.

MORRISBURG.

After passing the point, Morrisburg comes into view on the left—the prettiest village in the Dominion of Canada. Look at its churches, public buildings, private residences, and hotels (the St. Lawrence Hall is kept by W. H. Mc- Gannon and Brother, and I can say cheerfully no better hotel in town), that greet the eye, for we are still in the Province of Ontario. At half past three o'clock we enter the Province of Quebec. You will have a good chance then to compare the difference between the two Provinces. Your especial attention is called to this now, that you may be prepared to scan the change you will not fail to observe Before reaching Morrisburg is Doran's Island, which was rented by Mr. Oz Doran of the St. Regis Indians for one dollar per year, and they come every year 60 miles to collect one dollar. Opposite Morrisburg is Dry Island, used for picnics, etc.

One hour from this point to the Long Sault Rapids. We speak of this here, for it is about dinner time, and if you are lucky enough to secure a seat at the first table you will lose no point of interest, for it is presumable you will finish within the hour.

THE CUISINE ON THE BOAT.

It will not be amiss here to state that the meals were formerly served on the American plan, and were served in the upper saloon, and to give you but a faint idea of the commotion created by the passengers when there was one more person on board than seats at the table would require a volume ten times this size to describe. Therefore, please excuse me if I relate by way of illustration what an eminent French writer said on the subject: " The waiters, like little puppets, would bob up serenely at any time and place, drop a dish or whatever the hand contained, and was as soon out of sight. This continued for about one hour, while we were seated back against the cabin wall, with just space enough for the waiter to pass between us and the table. When the signal was given everybody made a rush for the table, and if the scene depicted could only be described humorously or otherwise I would like to read it." But the writer said it reminded him of the famous picture in her Majesty's gallery, "'The Rape of the Sabines." (I have never seen the picture, but presume it is that of a beautiful female poised as a central figure, and about ten soldiers ready to embrace her on a given signal.) Things have changed, however, and this season the meals will be served on the American plan, run by the company, who have secured the best stewards, etc., to superintend the service to the end, that everyone may be pleased. The upper saloon will not be used, but what was formerly known as the ladies' cabin will be the dining-room, which gives the whole saloon as a promenade and place of repose and rest for the passengers. I am positive the change will be acceptable.

About a mile below Morrisburg, on the right, is Gooseneck Island, so called from its resemblance to the neck of a goose ; the upper end is the neck ; the narrative is about nine miles long. Five miles from Morrisburg to

CHRYSLER'S FARM,

memorable for the battle fought on this ground in the year 1813. The Americans were the attacking party on this occasion, having arisen early in the morning, crossed the river into the little bay, landed, and immediately gone into the contest by attacking the little house. The fight was desperate, lasting until eleven o'clock, when the Americans, under General Williams, were repulsed with great slaughter. The house was completely riddled with bullets. It has since been torn down, and the chimney left as a monument to the battle. They retreated in good order, re-crossed the river, and remained, having abandoned the trip to Montreal which they intended. I draw this mild, because I am one of "God's people" myself.

Next in interest is Farron's Point, opposite which is Croyl's Island. Six minutes from here to Long Sault Rapids ; we pass on the left Harrison's Landing.

LONG SAULT ISLAND.

At this point there are really two channels, the American channel being on the right of Long Sault Island, the rapids forming the Canadian channel, and are on the left of the island. The distinguishing feature about the American channel is while it is swift in current, it has no rapids worthy of note, and the channel is used for tows, etc., and all the rafts naturally prefer this way, because it would be impossible for them to go down the Long Sault.

In the distant front observe a light-house at the head of the Cornwall canal. This canal is twelve miles in length, and passes around the Long Sault Rapids.

The boats are steered from landmarks on shore; by that small ball you see on the end of the pole, which is the bowsprit. The target that you see in the distance is used by the pilot to get his position in Long Sault Rapids. These targets will be seen frequently as you progress, and as they all answer the same purpose, this reference to them will suffice.

LONG SAULT RAPIDS.

Dickinson's Landing on the left was formerly a very important point on this line, as it was the foot of navigation before the canal was completed some forty years ago. Few changes have taken place since, that are apparent to the eye. The Long Sault is the first one of the first-class rapids, and the third one in line proceeding down the river, and as we set a price on the other two, you can set your own price on this one. A description of these rapids has been given from time immemorial; it does not behoove us to give any graphic or colored description of this scene, although we might do so satisfactorily, having seen depicted on the countenances of thousands of passengers who have passed this way everything in nature from the sublime to the ridiculous as well as between the two, and as each individual's feelings differ, no one description would do the subject justice. One writer said, "it was like sliding down hill on a steamboat." Another said he felt as if he was being *unglued!* A third said he felt as if he had taken a large dose of epecac. Still another as if he was on a ship at sea in a storm. And yet one more was so exhilerated that he imagined he owned Maud S. and would like to spend his days on the rapids. Another party who had ridiculed the trip a good deal, until the spray began to cover the deck, wetting them to the skin, drenching their store clothes, which, when dried, revealed awkward misfits, exclaimed that "it was the grandest sight they ever witnessed."

AN INCIDENT WORTHY OF NOTE

Occurred at this point on the right hand side of the rapids. Mr. Isaac Johnson and wife, of Spuyten Duyval, N. Y., and some friends were in the habit of coming to this section once every year, (as he also is at a great many other places in this country), which is noted for its fishing, being quite an enthusiast in the art. His guide, however, this year had built a new boat much larger than of previous years, consequently they ventured a little farther into the boiling caldron of remorseless strife and were upset, (just take a view of the position dear reader,) lucky for Mr. Johnson he always carries a rubber bag which he uses for a cushion whenever he is required to sit long in a boat, being a heavy man as well as tall. His first thought was to grasp the cushion, which acted as a life preserver; his wife clung to his neck, which forced him under water and in order to get breath he forced the cushion under water which allowed his head to appear above the wave and current, in this way they floated two miles and were rescued by the guide and boat coming along, and with clasped hands over the overturned boat were towed to shore. Mr. Johnson became blind and fainted from exhaustion, his plucky little wife was as firm and cool as a soldier under fire.

I could enlarge upon other descriptions, but prefer to give the Phat Boy a privilege to relate a few facts—no "taffy." All the boats of this line are built of Bessemer steel or iron, with three and one-half inches of elm rivited close to the iron on the bottom outside to prevent accidents if we should strike against a rock. This precaution was found necessary, because the first iron boat that struck a rock became a total wreck. With the protection of elm no injury has resulted from the occasional striking of the boats against the rocks. There is no danger, however, in this rapid, for the water in the shallowest place is thirteen and one-half feet, and we are drawing about seven feet. During our passage through all the rapids, we have four men at the wheel, and four men at the tiller aft, who assist the men at the wheel. Any accident that should happen to the chain or the wheel, the pilot immediately goes to the right hand of the tiller.

The Long Sault rapid is nine miles in length ; three miles of boisterous commotion : six miles of current and sudden, sharp turns. When we first enter the rapid, the steam on board of the boat is slowed down until she gets her position in the rapids, as she draws less water than when under full head of steam. We are then compelled to put on full steam as the boat must go faster than the current in order to obtain steerage way. Many suppose that no steam is used through the rapids, which is an error. If we were to attempt to go down without any propelling power, we would be at the mercy of the current of this stupendous agitation called rapids. One couldn't tell which end of the boat would be first, and it is presumable that this would be anything but pleasant to the passenger, for he would go down the same as a log, no one could tell which end of the boat would be first, anything but pleasure to passengers.

When we first enter this rapid, the finest view is obtained on the right side of the boat. It is expected, however, that the passengers will distribute themselves equally on either side to keep the boat in good trim; the Captain generally uses the "Phat Boy" for this purpose; when he is not on board, the passengers are expected to distribute themselves. The view, however, soon changes to the left, and when nearing the point, the swell and white caps run from seven to eleven feet in height.

We have already explained the causes of the rapids. Now, will any one please explain to me what is the height of the rocks which create this commotion, and at the same time set their price on this rapid. After passing this point and the swell and white caps that we have been describing, on the left is the passage to the Canadian channel of this river, which forms Barnhardt's island. On the right is the American channel. This was formerly used by boats before they came down the Long Sault, which for a long time was known as the lost channel. This channel having been lost for some years it was discovered by Captain Rankin, who received for that service a magnificent silver watch, the value of which at the present day would be about $6.50.

The first steamboat of this line that passed through the Long Sault, was the Passport, in 1847, and the pilot was W. H. McGanon, who is still in the employ of the company. The soundings were made by scows and rafts, with poles attached to the sides, of 8 to 15 feet in length, and as either of these met an obstruction and became dislodged or broken off, the depth of water was ascertained and a record made. The propelling power of these scows or rafts was oars or large paddles, worked by from 10 to 40 men as the necessities of each required.

The steamer Gill was the first boat through the rapids, and went down more by accident than otherwise, but it demonstrated the certainty of a channel.

Barnhardt's island on the left, $7\frac{1}{2}$ miles in length by $4\frac{1}{2}$ miles in width, belongs to the United States. On the right is the main land, St. Lawrence county, N. Y. Both sides of the river for the next seven miles belong to the United States. The King of Holland, who was the arbitrator of the treaty of 1812, from charts, maps, etc., furnished him, supposed that the main channel of the river passed around that island on the left. He was mistaken, however; this is the main channel of the river, and the only navigable one; the Canadian channel containing only about $3\frac{1}{2}$ or 4 feet of water.

During the next eight minutes we pass three very sudden turns in the river; the first turn is to the right; then to the left; next to the right again; the second turn being the sharpest on the St. Lawrence river; at direct angles turning to the left. Passengers on the left side of the boat, by looking backward, have a fine view of that portion of the river we have just passed, and looking forward see where we are compelled to go, and more easily note the sharpness of the turn. Rafts entering the American channel at the foot of the Long Sault rapids will drift nine miles in forty minutes, and are often thrown on shore on either side in making this sudden turn. After making our next turn to the right, by looking in the distance front, between the narrow point, will discover what is known as "The Crab." The current crosses here from right to left, then left to right, and from right to left forming the letter Z. Rafts get entangled in this portion of the river, and are easily torn to pieces.

There is a ferry boat plys between this point, on the right Macenia point and Cornwall point on the left, touching at two places on Barnhardt's island, to convey passengers who are desirous of visiting Macena Springs, six miles distant. The steamboat is a side-wheeler, two horses tread the power that revolves the wheels ; it is therefore a two-horse power boat ; they convey the steam on board in a bag well filled with oats. The deck hand is the cook ; the cook is the engineer ; the engineer is the mate, and the mate is the captain ; one man supreme command ; no mutiny ever occurs, unless the mule should kick the deck hand overboard—that would be a "*mulity*," would it not?

On the left is the entrance to the Canadian channel at the end of Barnhardt's island. Two miles below on the right is the last of the American shore on the St. Lawrence, lat. 45° N. Some few years ago I was presented by Messrs. W. H. Merrill & Co., 88 St. James St., Montreal, one of the dry goods firms in the city, with an American flag, fifteen feet in length, to designate the last of the United States shore on this river. Through the assistance of a friend at Cornwall, and thirteen dollars in cash, I succeeded in getting the flag in position. It remained there for about ten days, when a party of St. Regis Indians, who occupy a reservation six miles distant the other side of the Island—four of them came over to the point, filled themselves full of "ice water," climbed up the flag-staff and took down the flag. They cut it up into three or four suits of clothes, and went around this vicinity for about a week as full as a boiled oyster, singing " Hail Columbia, right side up," rolled up in the Stars and Stripes, full of fire-water, was said to be the happiest moment of their lives, and I have no reason to doubt it.

That portion of the river on the right is the dividing line for five miles; afterwards an iron fence or posts, set at equal distance apart, mark the boundary line. The river passing around that way forms Cornwall Island, about six miles wide. Rafts enter this portion of the river where the Racket River empties in, and are here refitted preparatory to being towed through the lake. Both sides of the river from this point downward belong to the Dominion of Canada.

In the distance, on the left is Cornwall, a village of 5,000 people, with the largest cotton and woolen mills in the Dominion. Since the protective tariff was inaugurated by the Dominion Parliament these industries have thrived wonderfully, and the town is correspondingly prosperous. Just before landing, a fine view is obtained of both the old and new Cornwall Canals. Looking at the old canal lock, and learning its dimensions, it is obvious why the steamers are their present size and no longer. These steamers are the limit which the locks will admit, hence if they were five feet longer or a trifle wider, they would be compelled to remain at Montreal, not being able to work through the locks. The new canal, which is alongside of the old one, will have locks 100 feet longer than the present one in use, consequently much larger boats will be able to ply the river. The old canal was considered amply large when built; it was not supposed that the travel on the St. Lawrence would ever reach its present and constantly increasing numbers.

After leaving Cornwall, on the right is Cornwall Island, 6 miles wide. Just beyond the island, on the right bank of the river, is St. Regis, an old Indian village, which cannot be seen from the deck of the steamer. But there is just one point where the church roof can be observed for a moment or so. There is, however, a tradition worth relating here: The bell hanging in this church is associated with a deed of genuine Indian revenge. On its way from France it was captured by an English cruiser and taken into Salem, Massachusetts, where it was sold to the church at Deerfield, in the same State. The Indians, hearing of the destination of their bell, set out for Deerfield, attacked the town, killed forty-seven of the inhabitants, and took 112 captives, among whom was the pastor and his family. The bell was then taken down and conveyed to St. Regis, where it now hangs.

During the next 10 miles of our trip the river is beautifully studded with Islands, and resembles the Thousand Islands scenery very much. Many of these islands are inhabited; some of them elegantly laid out with drives, etc. Rev. Mr. Dickinson's, called after himself, has a dock, at which steamers of this size can land; it has a hotel, number of cottages, and is quite a gay place in summer. On the left is Summers Town, beyond which is Hamilton's Island. Just before reaching Summers Town is the residence of Captain Cameron, of the Cultivature of this line; beyond is the magnificent villa of Hon. Caribou Cameron, the finest on the St. Lawrence. It is built of Ohio freestone, and cost $80,000. Hamilton Island, on the left, is occupied every summer by camping parties, who come from great distances, even from Virginia and Ohio, and remain two, three, and even four months. Day after day, one of their principal amusements is rowing out in their small boats, awaiting the arrival of the steamers, and then swiftly riding on top of the swell that is occasioned by the wheels of the steamer. The scene is exciting and picturesque On the right, we have now a fine view of the Adirondack Mountains of northern New York, and beyond the Green Mountains of Vermont, except it be a smoky or misty day, when the view is slightly obscured. It is 56 miles from the river to the mountains, and intervening is the wilderness of the State of New York, known as the John Brown tract, more famous as the hunting ground of adventurous gunning and fishing parties.

Continuing our course, we pass three small islands and enter Lake St. Francis, 28 miles in length—a very picturesque sheet of water indeed; but the trip through the lake is quite monotonous, therefore, for the next two hours, the guide, as well as the passengers, can "take a rest." This being a favorite route for honeymoon parties, there is now two full hours for these couples to enjoy the "honey" or the "moon," as seemeth to them best. After making this announcement one day, 53 left the deck; one, however, was an old bachelor, who went to curl his hair.

BOYS ON A STEAMER.

Here is a genuine. His parents are with him; he cannot keep still; he wants chiefly to break his neck or fall overboard, or to get crushed by the walking-beam; he has been twice dragged from the steps leading to the walking-beam, used by the assistant engineer for lubricating purposes; he would like to get in the paddle boxes, has talked every officer on board to death, and is now trying his best to worry the deck hands. How curiously constructed is a real boy, to go whither he should not, and especially where his anxious mother most fears he will go; he is now doing his best to spoil his parents trip. We can leave him for a moment; he won't flag in his endeavor to get into trouble or to make his parents miserable.

This is a smaller boy—not yet out of his petticoats, but very active; he, too, has with him an anxious mother; he has found another boy—a strange boy—of the same size and sex; they have become acquainted; the strange boy is allowed by his parents to roam about the boat at will; he invites the nice little boy to roam also; he wants him to roam as near the walking-beam as possible; he has roamed there himself before and escaped; he tells the nice little boy how cunning it is to come near being crushed; the nice little boy's mother forbids any roaming at all; she looks with disfavor on the strange boy; but the strange boy continues to hang around; he knows, so does the nice boy, together they can fool any one mother ; united they stand, divided they fall ; now the nice boy edges away from the side of his mother, for her energies are momentarily concentrated on the set of her bonnet and the nice-looking gentleman at the other end of the saloon who is taking side glances at her through the mirror. Now the nice boy gets farther away; they are on the forbidden part of the deck, near the walking beam. It is great fun. Now the cross man who keeps order on the deck drives them away. They go to the news agent's stand and help themselves to anything on the table when he is not looking. They are now running in and out of the state rooms, where the passengers have gone to take a little rest, getting in everybody's way ; it is a wonder they haven't been killed twenty times. It is great fun for the boys, but almost death to the passengers. And the mother is still so occupied with her bonnet and the dude who has made a mash or favorable impression upon her that she has not missed her nice little boy.

In the center of the lake, on the left, is the village of Lancaster, an old Scotch settlement. Just before reaching the village, what appears to be a stack of hay, but what is commonly known throughout Scotland as a Cairn. It is no more or less than a heap of stones in a rounded or conical form, placed in that way to commemorate some especial historic event. This one was built by the Glengarry Highlanders in 1847, to perpetuate the memory of Sir John Colburn, who was Commander-in-Chief of the Army and Governor-General of the Province. It was built by putting cobble-stones one on top of the other—each individual inhabitant or stranger passing that way adding a stone. See

Queen Victoria's Book, where she describes helping to build a Scotch Cairn with the assistance of John Brown, and one will get a better idea of how to build a Cairn. The county in which this place is located is named Glengarry, and is mainly or almost wholly inhabited by the sturdy Scotch highlanders, whose farms are of the finest in the Dominion. This is the last English speaking village on the route.

Passing three lighthouses, showing that the channel across the lake is quite intricate, we leave St. Anisette on the right, a small French town. We are now approaching the boundary line between the provinces of Ontario and Quebec. The lighthouses on either side show the geographical divisions. From the lighthouse on the left the line runs straight to the Ottawa river ; then the Ottawa becomes the dividing line. Just before arriving at the foot of the lake, where the river re-forms, we pass San Zotique ; next Coteau landing, where we call for the purpose of taking on a pilot,

EDWARD WILLETT,

whose duty it is to pilot this line of boats through the next series of rapids. We are coming to four rapids : first, the Coteau ; second, Cedar ; third, Split Rock, and fourth, the Cascades. The Canada Atlantic Railroad running from Ottawa, the capital of the Dominion, to Coteau Landing, the railroad ferry at this point conveys whole trains to Valley Field, where connections are made for Boston and New York—the shortest route from the capital to those points. On the extreme right at the foot of the lake is the village of Valley Field. It is at the head of the Beauhornias Canal, $11\frac{1}{2}$ miles in length, which passes around this series of rapids. The river, in 11½ miles, has a fall of 84 feet. The finest water power privilege on the continent of America, except Niagara, is at this point. The largest cotton mill in the Dominion, the Canada Paper Co's mill, and several other manufacturing establishments are located at Valley Field. After leaving St. Francis Lake, we re-enter the river. With our pilot we go down the small rapid known as the Coteau, passing Prisoner's island on the left, and on the left bank is the old French village of Coteau du Lac. On the extreme left at the point is an old French fort, where battles were fought in 1812 and 1813 ; the earthworks are still in a good state of preservation, behind which is the old saw-mill. Twenty minutes (or five miles) from this point to the Cedar rapids, then you will see der Rapid that is a Rapid, the most Rapid Rapid of all the Rapids, opposite the rapid is the village of Cedar on the left and St. Timothy on the right, the Cedar rapid the finest upon the St. Lawrence River. Look at St. Timothy, bear in mind the view you had of Morrisburg ; the impression of its beauty and thrift, and now you have the comparison. How does the former strike you as against the latter? It is a historic fact, and worthy of note, that no matter what town you arrive at in the province of Quebec, this will be apparent to the eye ; the finest buildings in the place will be the church, nunnery, school, hospital or priest's residence. Aside from these, the rest are all about alike. You cannot tell the palace residence from the blacksmith's shop, or the grocery store from the hotel. The church at St. Timothy has a seating capacity of 1,500 ; the population of the village is 600 ; the church is always full on Sundays, and as Mark Twain exclaimed, " What large domes these worshippers must have to their pantaloons for 600 to fill a place capable of seating 1,500." But they come from all the country around, being all of one persuasion. An opposition church is so far unknown in these rural parts, hence it may be inferred what the extraordinary power of this old church must be in the lower province.

Speaking to one of the priests one day regarding the amount of money collected by them from the poor to build and maintain their institutions, I asked him how it was, and he remarked that the millions have more money than the millionaires, and by getting the dollar from the poorer classes they had the million, which the millionaires never give up.

Just before arriving at St. Timothy, we enter the Cedar rapid and pass a distance of three and one-half miles in the extraordinary short time of seven minutes. By casting your eye shoreward, while passing an island on the left, and just before we enter the heaviest part of the rapid, you will discover how fast the boat is going. Looking to the right, you will see Hell's hole, and the greatest commotion in the river from Kingston to the Gulf.

Leaving Cedar rapid which is the most picturesque and beautiful (in our estimation) of all, two and one-half miles further along, and passing Bockey Hayes' shoal, which is a peculiar formation in the bed of the river, making navigation somewhat dangerous. In illustration : one day the steamer Corsican suddenly lurched to the left, and evidently struck a rock, whereupon the captain said to the pilot, " Edward, you are a little too far over to the left." Before he could complete the sentence, the boat lurched to the right and struck another rock; then the pilot replied, "yes, and a little too far over to the right side. It is plain that the channel about here is at least precarious. The government engineers, however, are now at work removing these dangerous obstructions. The Napoleon hats you see in the distance, on poles about ten feet high, are the marks which enable the pilot to obtain his true bearings through the shoal. Turning to the right we come in sight of the Split Rock rapid, the most dangerous rapid of all. When we speak of danger, we don't mean to life or limb, as no person was ever injured on this rapid; it is danger to property that we refer to, as this is the only one of the series that has cost the company one dollar. They lost one steamboat here, and have had others upon the rocks. On the 8th of July, 1874, the steamer Corinthian, of the R. O. N. Co., when passing the Split Rock rapid, was almost instantly enveloped by a terrific thunder shower, accompanied by a hurricane. The wind was so powerful that the boat refused to answer the helm, and instead of turning to the right, as she should, the wind caused her to go straight ahead, and we struck a rock forward about five feet high and passed fifteen feet aft of the wheel over the same, and then stopped. I was upon the right hand side of the boat explaining to the passengers and showing or pointing out to them the ledge of rock when she struck. Immediately four ladies caught hold of me (whom they thought was the boss life preserver). What a position for a nice young man. I was about to exclaim as my friend A. Ward did when he was surrounded by 20 of Brigham Young's wives, "I hope your intentions are honorable." However, through the assistance of some friends, I procured life preservers for them and was released from my somewhat precarious position. In a space of an hour most of the passengers were landed by the aid of the ship's boats and battaus from the shore, and proceeded by rail to Montreal, where they arrived the same evening. I remained on board all night until a derrick was erected and two of the boats lashed together, and a platform built upon them, when I was let down by the aid of the derrick upon the same, and without further trouble taken to shore in safety. The second line of white-caps which you see in the distance in front, is the Split Rock, a ledge of rock running from shore to shore, with the exception of a break of about sixty feet, which is a natural split in the rock. Formerly there was only a depth of nine feet of water; it was blasted out, and now gives a navigable channel of thirteen and one-half feet. Passengers, by looking into the water on the right side of the boat, can see the ledge we have been talking about.

One and a half miles from here to the Cascade, the last of this series of four, and the last but one on the river—the Lachine being the last. The Cascade differs from all the rest, being a cutting, chopping sea, in which the boats are wrenched more than in any other rapid. On the right is the village of Melocheville, at the foot of the Beauhornois canal, eleven and one-half miles in length, that passes around this line of rapids. The boats of this and all other lines are compelled to pass through this canal, as none of them could ascend this line of rapids.

We are now thirty miles by water and twenty-four miles by land from Montreal. In the distance in front, is Mount Royal or Montreal mountain. The park mountain drive, the most famous drive in the world, is up the brow of this mountain through a park. On the left is Il Perot Island, formed by the two channels of the Ottawa. The one we now see comes by St. Anns, where Moore wrote his famous Canadian boat song. A resident of St. Anns, Lieutenant-Colonel Dowker, says that every spring the freshets of the Ottawa cause the water to come down into the St. Lawrence with such force as to cause an eddy to pass up the point of the island and pass down the navigable channel of the Ottawa, and he can take a pail from his house, Chateau Blanc (where the famous poet Moore resided while at St. Anns and wrote his Canadian poems), proceed down to the river and dip up a pail of pure clear St. Lawrence water. Meeting Col. Dowker last spring, he told me that the freshets of the Ottawa in March and April, 1885, were the most alarming and disastrous ever known. The sudden breaking up of the ice caused a jam. Houses were moved from their foundations, cattle and sheep crushed to jelly by the ice and many drowned; the ice piled mountains high. The government had an agent in the vicinity relieving the distressed inhabitants. The heavy flow of ice by the freshets in the Ottawa caused a jam a little below Montreal this year, consequently flooded the city, causing much damage to life and property. The oldest church in the upper Province and old forts are to be seen here.

On the left a portion of the Ottawa empties into the St. Lawrence. This is not, however, the main channel; the navigable portion of the river is just the other side of Il Perot. Note the difference between the color of the two waters; they are as wide apart as green is from purple. The water of the Ottawa is of a dark brown color, caused by passing over low, marshy, peat bed soils, and the huge forests through which this river passes, the leaves falling and rotting, and swept along by the freshets, doubtless dye the water to the peculiar color observable. The waters of the two rivers do not readily mix, and each are distinct for many miles.

In the distance is Lake St. Louis, or Lachine Lake, 15 miles from the rapids to the foot of the lake, where we arrive at Lachine, on the left, and Caughnawaga on the right. The latter is the residence of the Indian pilot, St. Jean Baptiste. who takes this line of boats down the Lachine Rapids.

About half way through the lake on the right we come to Nun's Island. That mound or elevation of ground which you see was a fort in 1812, and English and American war-like parties met in sanguinary contest around here. It commands the entrance to the Chateaugay River. The village of Chateaugay is about 6 miles back. The Nun's Island belongs to the Grey Nuns, of Montreal, who have a hospital for their own sick, and the spot is marked by a large cross emblematic of their order.

Fifteen minutes from here we are in sight of Caughnawaga, where we take on board the Indian pilot, who has become of historical interest to tourists, as it was he who discovered the channel and took the first of this line down, August 19, 1840, and has been in the employ of the company ever since. He is 70 years old, weighs 240 pounds, and stands 6 feet high. Many of the passengers imagine he is the only pilot who can take a boat through the Lachine Rapids. This is not correct, for we have other pilots who can; but as he is paid for this especial service, they resign most cheerfully in his favor. He has never had an accident; and the company believe in holding to that which is good, and therefore "stick to the old man." He will emerge from shore in a small boat, accompanied by his two sons. They row him to the steamers; he comes on board, and the boys row home again. He remains on board till the next morning, takes the first train for Lachine, where he is met by the boys, who take him home in the row-boat. The Indian pilot's name is St. Jean Baptiste de Lisle; his Indian name, Ta ya ka, meaning in the U. S. language that "he will cross the river," but does not; he goes down the rapids. He has a family of six children, three boys and three girls. The girls are unmarried. I state this for the benefit of the young men on board, as the Indian pilot says he wants a "heap Yankee" for his girls. I am engaged to my Mary Jane, and they can't have me.

Here the Indian pilot comes on board—a description of Caughnawaga would not be amiss. Note the line of palatial residences along the bank beyond the church, the windows and doors kicked out to give them light and air, the palace gardens in the front part of the back end of the house. The laundry of Caughnawaga is usually hung on the fence; it is not wash day to-day, as you can perceive. The bathhouse is the whole water-front, but it is seldom used. The water-works is that barrel on the shore. The fair damsel waving her lily white hand is Mary Jane, my best girl. She comes out every day to welcome me, as she thinks I am on board. You can get her eye and have a flirtation, the same as I have had for years, and not make me jealous. That large brick structure is the centennial building, built during the centennial year by the celebrated Indian Chief, White Kicker. I think they use him to kick the windows and doors out of the palatial residences previously spoken of.

Caughnawaga, signifying "Praying Indian" (my friend Ben Butler says they spell it with an e), is well laid out for an Indian village, with a population of 900, all Indians; no whites can live here.

The finest crops raised in this section of the country are raised just below Caughnawaga. They raise them with a derrick. It is a blasted crop, however, and of no use until it is. This notable quarry is where most of the stone comes from for the construction of the locks in the new Lachine Canal—the entrance of which is at Lachine, the village just passed at the foot of the lake on the left.

THE VILLAGE OF LACHINE

is a favorite resort for Montrealers in summer. The inhabitants number about 2,000, but it is frequently augmented in the season to 9,000 or 10,000. Note the large buildings, which are the church, Villa de Marie Convent, the School and University for the education of priests.

Our Indian pilot being on board, he will now show his Injin-uity in piloting a boat down the Lachine Rapids. Before reaching the rapids, the tourist can see the aqueduct that supplies the city of Montreal with water.

THE LACHINE RAPIDS

differ from all the rest; it is simply an intricate channel through rock. Take your position upon either side of the boat and you will know when we come to the most important point, as the boat will be headed direct for a little island, which is nothing more nor less than a few loads of dirt upon a huge ledge of rock. Keep your eye upon the bow of the boat and you will be led to exclaim, why we are going to strike the island; and if you are a betting person or a truthful one, you would almost swear we could not help but strike; but when within less than ten feet we make a very sudden turn to the right, with a grand pitch or lurch, in which you will think the boat drops ten feet. We pass alongside of a ledge of rocks for about half a mile, to see which you must be upon the right hand side of the boat; at the end of this ledge of rock we have a perfect miniature Niagara, a little water-fall for a cent. Do not allow the lurching of the boat from side to side, to cause you any uneasiness as there is no danger, because a side wheel boat has guards from four to ten feet projecting over on each side from the hull, 60 to 90 feet long, so that when that flat surface strikes the water by lurching that is as far as she can go, therefore, will always righten herself immediately. I have had a great deal of sport in this way. When the boat had lurched over as far as she could I would immediately exclaim: "Oh! I am on the wrong side," and proceed to the high side, when the boat would immediately righten up and the passengers would think I did it, but she would have rightened without my aid. Yet I have heard some very strong-minded women, after seeing the effect of my moving to the high side of the boat, exclaim: "Put that big man off; he has too much weight to be upon a boat in the rapids" This is the last rapid built on the St. Lawrence, you can have it the best one if you like and I will not

FAMOUS FOR ONE-THIRD OF A CENTURY.

THE ST. LAWRENCE HALL,

MONTREAL.

Is so arranged that rooms used for guests are only one flight above the **GRAND OLD PARLORS,** which are just one flight of stairs from St. James Street. This item of rooms below the clouds, with plenty of light and air, is worthy of attention. The new Ladies' Entrance, Grand Drawing Room Parlors and Suits of Rooms just added, the last furnished, therefore the best in the city.

THE ST. LAWRENCE HALL

Occupies a frontage on St. James Street 180 feet, on St. Francis Xavier Street 145 feet, on Craig Street 180 feet, and on St. George Street 110 feet, in the very heart of the city, opposite the new Post Office. Thus

From $2 to $5 is Saved from Hack Hire Alone.

The only first-class hotel located within one mile of the Post Office and all the public buildings. Its table, unequalled by any in the Dominion. The Hotel is supplied with Cream, Milk, Butter and Vegetables from its own farm, fresh every day.

Only one block from the French Cathedral. Two blocks from Victoria Square. Only two blocks from the Theatre Royal. Within two blocks of all the Business and Dry Goods Palaces.

The nearest first-class Hotel to the depots and steamboat landings. Every place worthy of note to the tourist is within fifteen minutes walk of the St. Lawrence Hall, except those you see in your Park Mountain Drive. This hotel was the home of all royal and notable personages who visited Montreal for thirty years. It has all the modern improvements, Elevator, Gas and Electric Lights, Hot and Cold Water, Electric Bells, Rooms En-Suite, with Bath and Closets on every floor. Spacious, clean and well ventilated rooms. The best beds of any hotel in the city. The prices are graduated. All under the personal supervision of

MR. HENRY HOGAN.

quarrel with you for it. All I ask you to do is to stop at the hotels who advertise in my book and tell them I was the cause, and if they do not treat you well I will proceed to sit down upon them, and they will never have occasion to treat any one else badly. Passing the foot of the rapids a first view of Montreal on the left, and on the right is the village of La Prairie. The first mountain on the left is Mount Bruno ; second, Belleisle ; the third, St. Pie. The next and last sensation on the trip is passing under

VICTORIA BRIDGE,

the largest and longest tubular bridge in the world ; was built by Mr. Stephenson in 1860 for the Grand Trunk Railroad, by which it is owned and controlled. It is a mile and three-quarters of iron, two miles and a quarter with its approaches from shore. It is wholly of iron, top, bottom and sides—an iron tunnel or box, as it were. There are twenty-four abutments, built wedge shaped (to crush the immense ice fields that pass through this section, which, previous to the building of the bridge, did immense damage to Montreal during the spring freshets. There are no such things as freshets on the St. Lawrence, the Ottawa flowing in some miles above causing such disasters), upon which rest the sections of iron. These spans are from 250 to 360 feet long each, and the center span is about 60 feet high. The bridge tubes are 16 x 22 feet. It contains no wagon road or foot path, and is used by the G T. R. and its connecting lines. The cost of this immense work was $6,250,000, about one half of which amount went to fatten the contractors. I was not one of them. I mention this on account of my size, and for fear some one might think I was wealthy.

The bridge is constructed of sheets of iron with a two-inch edge turned up and riveted to each other. It is fastened to the center, loose on both ends on rollers, and is provided with a sliding track, so that there is no danger by expansion or contraction to passing trains. It expands and contracts from three and one half to seven inches. The bridge is kept in thorough repair and well painted. The small holes, or perforations, in the sides of the bridge were originally intended to convey the smoke out, but found inadequate for that purpose ; therefore, they caused to be erected a line of flues the whole length. Now if any smoke remains it is carried out in a hand basket. The two movable scaffolds you see are used by the workmen in repairing and painting. It is not a draw bridge, and as we pass under the center span, and not over it, you need not remove your hat if you remain on the deck. After passing under the bridge you will have a magnificent view of

MONTREAL HARBOR.

The points of interest in the harbor will all be described to you as we pass over St. Lambert's shoal, a very dangerous passage, previous to landing at the Quebec boat, where we transfer such passengers as desire to visit Quebec. The island you see front on the right is St. Helen's Isle, used by the citizens of Montreal for pleasure, picnic parties, etc. A ferry plys between the city and island every half hour, from morning until 7 p m. On Sunday from 3,000 to 20,-000 persons visit the island, mostly French Canadians, three-fifths of whom comprise the population of Montreal. In the distant front on the left is the oldest church in Montreal ; to the left of that, the largest building with the dome, is the Bonseccour Market and old City Hall. The new City Hall is that large building in the rear with the dome in the center and four columns—one in each corner. Across the road to the left, that long building is the Court House. At the head of Jacques Cartier Square is a magnificent column erected to the memory of Admiral Lord Nelson. At the foot of the square lies a steamer of the Richelieu and Ontario Navigation Company. There are two steamers on this line, notably, the *Montreal* and *Quebec*. This company own twenty-one side-wheel boats. The Quebec line has the largest boats that float the St. Lawrence River ; they will compare favorably with the boats of the Sound or the Hudson River—triple-decked palace boats, built of Bessemer steel ; one has a capacity of 360 state rooms—the other 280. The distance to Quebec is 180 miles, and the fare on this line is only $2.50—the cheapest on the continent. Beyond, on the left, the two massive towers you see belong to the French church of Notre Dame. It is not a Cathedral, but simply a parish church. (The Cathedral is on Dominion Square, in process of erection, and when complete, will be one-half the size of St. Peter's at Rome). It is the largest on the continent, and has contained within its walls front porch and stairways, on the 24th of June last (St. John's day), twenty-two thousand souls. Beyond is the Custom House, with the clock in the tower, and still further up the examining warehouse of the Custom House, as well as the office, docks and steamers of the Allen line. The first stop is at Quebec boat ; passengers for Montreal remain on deck, as this line is compelled to enter the first lock in the Lachine canal ; the gates close and the water is allowed to

For Comfort, Safety and Convenience, Choose In Traveling,

EAST OR WEST,

THE CENTRAL VERMONT
RAILROAD,

WHICH FORMS ITS CONNECTION WITH THE

GRAND TRUNK RAILWAY.

The Old and Favorite New England Route.

TO AND FROM ALL POINTS WEST.

The Rolling Stock and Equipment of the CENTRAL VERMONT R. R. is second to no road in the country. It is the only line running

PULLMAN SLEEPING CARS

Between Chicago and Boston without change, and solid trains of Elegant Coaches and Baggage Cars, without change between Montreal and Boston.

Steel Rails, Iron Bridges, with Westinghouse Air Brakes, Miller Pla'form. Coupler and Buffer on every train, assures safety while passing swiftly through Mountain, Lake and River Scenery of the most beautiful and varied description.

The train service of this road is so arranged that sure connections are made with the Grand Trunk Railway, and with railroads in New England to and from all the principal cities, towns and villages in

Massachusetts, Rhode Island, Connecticut and Vermont.

Wagner Cars, Montreal to New York without change, Pullman Palace Cars run to Boston via this Line.

Also first-class Restaurants with reasonable charges, and ample time given for meals.

☞ Baggage checked through Canada in Bond, avoiding all trouble of Customs.

During the summer, EXCURSION TICKETS are sold over this line at greatly reduced rates. Ask for rates via this line before buying, and note that your tickets read via CENTRAL VERMONT RAILROAD, for sale at all Stations and responsible Ticket Offices, East and West.

COMPANY'S OFFICES—260 Washington Street, Boston; 317 Broadway, New York; 136 St. James Street, Montreal.

A. C. STONEGRAVE, Agent, 136 St. James Street, Montreal.

J. W. HOBART, General Manager.

S. W. CUMMINGS, General Passenger Agent.

General Office, St. Albans, Vt.

enter, which raises the boat to the level of the lock when the passengers are allowed to depart. Montreal is the commercial metropolis of the Dominion, with a population of 150,000, three-fifths of which are French Canadians. The docks, piers, wharfs, etc., of Montreal are the finest on the continent. It is the second city of commercial importance —New York being first. Six steamship companies leave here weekly for Europe during the summer season and a large amount of business must of a necessity be done, as its channel is closed during five months of the winter. The water front is all lighted with the electric light, so that work is carried on during the summer months night and day. Having selected your hotel and arrived at the same, our next duty will be to see the sights of

MONTREAL.

It is situated at the head of navigation for ocean vessels, 540 miles from the Gulf of St. Lawrence, on the Island of Montreal, which lies between the two great rivers of the North, the St. Lawrence and the Ottawa. The island is about thirty two miles in length, and at its widest some ten in breadth; it is so fertile as to be called the garden of the Province. The surface of the land is level with the exception of the eminence of Mount Royal, which rises 550 feet above the river level. Mount Royal gives the name to the city which lies at its base. The settlement of the town was originally determined by the first explorer, Jacques Cartier, in 1535, at which time an Indian village, Hochelaga, occupied the spot. The permanent founding of the place, however, did not occur until 1642, and in one hundred years of growth thereafter it gathered a population of 4,000. It was under French rule until 1760, when it passed into the hands of the British. In 1832 the cholera raged in Montreal with great violence, carrying off 1,843 inhabitants in a population of about 30,000. In April, 1849, a political mob burnt the Parliament buildings, which were erected on McGill street, and the seat of Government was, in consequence, transferred to Quebec, thence to Toronto, and finally to Ottawa, where it remains. In July, 1852, a destructive fire laid waste a large portion of the city, burning 110 houses, and consuming property valued at $1.400,000. Notwithstanding these reverses the city recovered, and to-day numbers a population of 150,000. Years of industry and enterprise have produced growth and improvement in Montreal, such as but few American cities can boast of, and perhaps but one—Chicago—has exceeded. At the beginning of the present century vessels of more than 300 tons could not ascend to Montreal, and its foreign trade was carried on by brigs and barges. Now ocean steamships of over 4,000 tons, the floating palaces of the Richelieu and Ontario Navigation Company, and ships of from 700 to 4,000 tons from all parts of the world, occupy the wharves of the harbor, which are not equaled on this continent in point of substantial construction, convenience and cleanliness. The old part of Montreal, near the river, has narrow incommodious streets; but the new growth of the city toward Mount Royal has been liberally laid out, with wide and cheerful thoroughfares. The architecture here is very fine; the material chiefly used is a zinc-colored lime-stone, extensively quarried three miles from the city. The public buildings, banks, and principal warehouses are solid and handsome enough to adorn a European capital. The great wealth of the Roman Catholic

Church has enabled it to erect many magnificent churches, hospitals and convents, always in a very massive and enduring style. Other denominations seem to have been excited by emulation, and vie with each other in the beauty and elegance of their places of worship. Among the evidences of the French origin of the city are to be noticed, a few curious old buildings to be found lingering here and there about Jacques Cartier Square, or occupying sites on the eastern part of the river front. The old houses are built somewhat like fortifications, and have heavily vaulted cellars, wherein treasure might be stored or a defense made against hostile foes, in the days when Indians and Whites, French and British were fighting and plundering each other. The French Canadians in the city, continue still to be a little more than half the population, and, although their language here has not been unaffected by the constant intercourse with English-speaking people, it is not, as commonly supposed, a *patois*, but such French as was spoken by the polite and educated in France, when the emigrants who first settled Canada, left the shore of their mother-land. The naming of many of the streets of Montreal after saints and holy things reminds one that its founders were not exiles nor adventurers but enthusiastic missionaries.

PLACES OF INTEREST.

The Post Office is built on St. James street, the chief throughfare of this city, opposite the new St. Lawrence Hall. The reason I use the word new may be asked. Well, the hotel has been newly re fitted, the corner building purchased, one hundred elegant and commodious rooms added

under French rule until 1760, when it passed into the hands of the British. In 1832 the cholera raged in Montreal with great violence, carrying off 1,843 inhabitants in a population of about 30,000. In April, 1849, a political mob burnt the Parliament buildings, which were erected on McGill street, and the seat of Government was, in consequence, transferred to Quebec, thence to Toronto, and finally to Ottawa, where it remains. In July, 1852, a destructive fire laid waste a large portion of the city, burning 110 houses, and consuming property valued at $1,400,000. Notwithstanding these reverses the city recovered, and to-day numbers a population of 150,000. Years of industry and enterprise have produced growth and improvement in Montreal, such as but few American cities can boast of, and perhaps but one—Chicago —has exceeded. At the beginning of the present century vessels of more than 300 tons could not ascend to Montreal, and its foreign trade was carried on by brigs and barges. Now ocean steamships of over 4,000 tons, the floating palaces of the Richelieu and Ontario Navigation Company, and ships of from 700 to 4,000 tons from all parts of the world, occupy the wharves of the harbor, which are not equaled on this continent in point of substantial construction, convenience and cleanliness. The old part of Montreal, near the river, has narrow incommodious streets; but the new growth of the city toward Mount Royal has been liberally laid out, with wide and cheerful thoroughfares. The architecture here is very fine; the material chiefly used is a zinc-colored lime-stone, extensively quarried three miles from the city. The public buildings, banks, and principal warehouses are solid and handsome enough to adorn a European capital. The great wealth of the Roman Catholic

Church has enabled it to erect many magnificent churches, hospitals and convents, always in a very massive and enduring style. Other denominations seem to have been excited by emulation, and vie with each other in the beauty and elegance of their places of worship. Among the evidences of the French origin of the city are to be noticed, a few curious old buildings to be found lingering here and there about Jacques Cartier Square, or occupying sites on the eastern part of the river front. The old houses are built somewhat like fortifications, and have heavily vaulted cellars, wherein treasure might be stored or a defense made against hostile foes, in the days when Indians and Whites, French and British were fighting and plundering each other. The French Canadians in the city, continue still to be a little more than half the population, and, although their language here has not been unaffected by the constant intercourse with English-speaking people, it is not, as commonly supposed, a *patois*, but such French as was spoken by the polite and educated in France, when the emigrants who first settled Canada, left the shore of their mother-land. The naming of many of the streets of Montreal after saints and holy things reminds one that its founders were not exiles nor adventurers but enthusiastic missionaries.

PLACES OF INTEREST.

The Post Office is built on St. James street, the chief throughfare of this city, opposite the new St. Lawrence Hall. The reason I use the word new may be asked. Well, the hotel has been newly re fitted, the corner building purchased, one hundred elegant and commodious rooms added

with baths and closets, electric bells and elevators, ladies'
reception room, new and elegantly furnished suits of rooms
added this year. The old proprietor, Mr. Hogan, pronounced by connoisseurs to be the best landlord in the Dominion, has assumed the proprietorship and has associated
with him as manager, Mr. Samuel Montgomery, the best
choice that could be made, as he is an American from the
Pacific slope, where they know how to keep a hotel. I
therefore cheerfully recommend you to stop at the new St.
Lawrence Hall during your stay in Montreal. Starting
from there, it being the centre, every point of interest is
within fifteen minutes' walk of this hotel. The first building
to the left is the new Post Office, recently finished, with
a richly decorated exterior, and every internal improvement which modern ingenuity has devised. Adjoining it
is the Bank of Montreal, in the Corinthian style of architecture, with a sculpture on the pediment depicting native
Indians, a sailor and settler with the emblems of the arts
and trade. The corporation occupying this noble building
is the richest one of the kind in America. It has branches
in every town of importance in the Dominion, and has offices in New York, Chicago and London. It issues letters of
credit on all parts of the world. Its capital and reserve
fund amount to $18,000,000. Adjoining the Bank of Mon-
treal is the Canada Pacific Railroad office, a simple solid
structure in the Doric style. Crossing the street a little
above the corner on the right hand side is 88 St. James street,
where W. H. Merrill & Co., have opened a new store for
the sale of silks, velvets, laces, gloves, silk underwear and
hosiery, they were formerly on Notre Dame street, but are
now established at 88 St. James street, where they would be

glad to meet their old customers and as many new ones. Other banks having their offices on Place d'Arms are the Jacques Cartier, Ontario, Quebec and National Banks. On the south side of the square the great parish church of Notre Dame looms up. The dimensions of this vast Norman edifice are 225 feet in length, and 134 feet in width. Its towers are 220 feet high; the western one contains the largest bell in America, " Gros Bourdon," in weight 29,400 pounds. The seating capacity of the church is 10,000. It has recently been decorated in deep colors and gold, after the manner of the St. Chapelle at Paris. Suspended over the western gallery, and near the grand altar, is an immense wooden crucifix. This was brought from France two centuries ago, and first set up in the church built on the ground now Place d'Arms. Adjoining Notre Dame is the venerable Seminary of St. Sulpice, with its old gateway, courtyard and clock. The gentlemen of this seminary originally held valuable rights affecting the entire island of Montreal; much of the land yet remains in their hands. With the wealth thus brought to their coffers they have liberally established and conducted many institutions of charity and education scattered throughout the city. We are now on Notre Dame street, the chief retail street in Montreal. Turning eastward a few feet from Notre Dame church, on the right is R. Sharpley & Sons, which will repay a visit; a cordial invitation is extended and I am sure it will be time well spent if you call. A little above on the left, 1671, J. & E. McEntyre, merchant tailors. They make all my clothes, therefore if they can fit me further comments are unnecessary. A little above is Lanthier & Co. Let us go on we shall soon arrive at the Court House, a fine Grecian building of simple and massive appearance. A few steps further on the right brings us to Nelson's monument, setting forth in bas-relief the various victories which the great naval hero won without the loss of a single British ship. This monument is in Jacques Cartier square, at the foot of which is the wharf of Quebec steamers.

Keeping on Notre Dame street, directly beside the monument, we find opposite to each other two buildings which form a sharp contrast. The one on the left is the new City Hall, a lofty and ornate specimen of French architecture; facing it is the " old chateau," a structure probably thought very fine a century ago, when Benjamin Franklin set up in it the first printing press ever used in the city. Now the old place is a Normal School, and the discoveries of the illustrious American is explained there, and let us hope his witty sayings repeated and acted upon. We can now take our way to the river side, and a block from Jacques Cartier Square shall find Bonsecours Market, a vast substantial Doric structure. Here, if it be market day, we may see a little of the French Canadian peasantry, clad in their homespun, and bargaining about their fowls, or eggs or butter with many queer words and phrases now almost forgotten in the Normandy whence they were first brought. Next to the market is Bonsecours Church, a rough-cast building with a high pitched roof and with a breadth of a few feet adjoining it, occupied by cobblers and cake shops. This church is the oldest Roman Catholic one in the city; its entrance is at the farther side; rarely is it unoccupied by some worshipers from the adjacent market, who bring in, without ceremony, their baskets and bundles. Suspended over the altar is a model of a ship in bright tin, in which usually burning tapers are placed. Returning, on the water-front, we note the ships and steamers from Liverpool, Glasgow, London, Havre, Rotterdam and other ports ; and on the right successively pass the Custom House, a triangular building, with a clock tower; the office of the Allen Line, also having a clock and the fine building of the Harbor Commissioners. Next to it is a curious looking pile, with external hoist-ways from top to bottom, this is the Customs Examining Warehouse. Before we leave this vicinity, we shall glance backward at the street from Allen's office to the Custom House.

Taking a short journey, still upon the river front, we come to the great works of stone masonry, which give to Montreal an enlarged canal to Lachine, so that vessels of much greater tonnage than the ones at present used may be employed in the grain trade. This enterprise is one of a series of canal improvements by which Canada strives to retain and increase its business as a highway for the shipment of western produce to the sea-board.

Retracing our steps, we take the wide street running up from the city, McGill, and mark the fine warehouses that adorn it. Arriving at Notre Dame street, a little above, on the left, John Murphy & Co., who invite you to inspect their stock, styles and prices. Adjoining is Mr. S. Carsley, who occupies the six or seven stores in succession, which you are invited to inspect, and I am positive you will be as favorably impressed as I was. Retracing our steps back to McGill street, we turn to the right, and immediately in front, just one block, is Victoria Square, which contains a statue of the Queen by Marshall Wood. Corner St. James street opposite, on the left, is the Albert Buildings. Turning to the right we enter St. James street. The first building of note on the right is the Ottowa Buildings, on the left is J. J. Milloy, the tailor, where tailor-made suits for ladies are a specialty. A little further on the right, is G. W. Clark, The Souvenir Palace, where, if you enter, the sight of such rare curiosities and splendid souvenirs will cause you to wonder how you got in without a ticket, and a little above is Drysdale & Co., where any religious book may be had, Seaside Library, stationery, etc. This is the largest bookstore in Canada and the most cheerful, as they have just added a waiting parlor, where you can meet a friend and visit " Alexander's" if you desire ; it is a little above on the left where is kept confections, "bons bons," etc., and you can be served with the best the market affords. On our way to the Post Office from whence we started. At the corner of St. Peter street is the Mechanics' Institute. This building contains a good library, the admission fee to which is only nominal, and a very good reading room, having on its tables the principal dailies of America, the London *Times*, the Glasgow *Herald*, the Dublin *Warder*, the Edinburgh *Scotsman*, and all the weeklies monthlies and quarterlies of both England and the United States. Strangers can have free access to this reading-room, for the period of two weeks, by applying to Mr. Hogan, the proprietor of the new St. Lawrence Hall.

Opposite to the Mechanics Institute is the Merchants' Bank, built in modern Italian style, with polished granite columns at the entrance ; the interior of this bank should be seen ; the man office is carried up two stories in height and is beautifully frescoed. Diagonally across the street is

Molson's Bank, also of Italian design, and richly decorated. We are now nearly at the hotel again, where we may conclude for the present our inspection of the city.

Resuming our sight-seeing, we shall now leave behind us the business streets, and take our way to the upper part of Montreal. Our suggestion is, take St. James street to the first crossing on the right as you leave the hotel, St. Peter street. After two blocks this street changes its name to Bleury street (when, if you find you are footsore, you can turn to the left to the end of the block, on Craig street, No. 1722, where is located the celebrated Surgeon Chiropodist, Prof. Harris, who will attend to any trouble of the feet, that will be sure to make your walk a pleasant one, provided you are, like me, suffering from corns, bunions or ingrowing nails). At No. 17 Bleury street, we may enter Notman's studio, a large handsome, building entirely devoted to photographic art. Here we may spend half an hour very pleasantly in looking over views of Canadian scenery, and portraits taken singly or skillfully grouped, representing the sports and pastimes of our winter. The chief of these pictures is that which shows a carnival held at the Victoria Skating Rink eight years ago, when H. R. H. Prince Arthur was present. This Photographic marvel, with others now surrounding it on the walls of Mr. Notman, attracted great attention and admiration at the Centennial Exhibition. Mr. Notman was photographer to the Exhibition and received it highest awards.

Continuing on Bleury street we soon reach, on the left, the Church of the Jesu, with St. Mary's College adjoining it, conducted by the Jesuit fathers. This church is modeled after one of the same name at Rome, where the remains of Loyola are entombed. The style of architecture is the round Roman arch. The interior is one of the most beautiful among American churches. Over the high altar is a fresco of the crucifixion. In the southern transcept the sufferings of the first Canadian martyr, burnt by savages, are depicted. Leaving the elegant house of prayer, we shall continue on Bluery street until we come to St. Catharine street. A few steps brings us to the Nazareth Asylum for the Blind, attached to which (No. 1091) is a most ornate chapel, decorated in such a lovely manner as to lead one to suppose that it was done to encourage the suffering inmates of the asylum to see.

The next building on the side of the street (No. 1077) is the Roman Catholic Commercial Academy, a lordly monument of wealth and munificence, containing all the modern appliances for the practical training of youth, and presided over by an able staff of professors. If we keep going eastward on St. Catherine street, we pass on St. Dennis street, the immense parish church of St. James, with the tallest spire in the city. Near by is the new church which is dedicated to Notre Dame De Lourdes ; water and relics from her shrine at Lourdes in France, are for sale in the basement. Adjoining the church are its conventual buildings.

Returning on St. Catherine street, we soon come to Christ Church Cathedral (Church of England), unquestionably the most beautiful specimen of Gothic architecture in Canada. It is of cruciform design ; its extreme width is 100 feet. The spire, which is entirely of stone, rises to the height of 224 feet. The materials of construction are Montreal limestone and stone from Caen, in Normandy, which latter, by exposure to the weather, has changed from almost pure whiteness to a yellow tint. On the grounds of the cathedral are erected the residences of the bishop and his assistants, the Synod Hall, and also a fine monument to Bishop Fulford, the first Metropolitan of Canada. The street running on the farther side of the cathedral is University street, and No. 82, one block distant, is the Natural History Museum, containing a good Canadian collection. University street leads us down to Dorchester street, on the corner of which is the St. James Club House. Taking Dorchester street eastward, we pass on the left St. Paul's Church (Presbyterian). On the same side we soon have a view of the vast proportions of the new Roman Catholic cathedral in course of construction.

Across the square on which St. Peter's is building, we notice a beautiful church, St. George's (Church of England), and adjoining it is its Sunday school, the largest and best conducted in Canada. On Dorchester street, fronting Dominion Square on Peel street, is the Windsor Hotel. Next beyond on Dorchester street is the Victoria Skating Rink, where immense carnivals are held in the winter—the grandest in the world. In the summer the spacious edifice is used for concerts, walking matches, public gatherings, meetings, etc. Two blocks distant is the Foundling Hospital of the Gray Nun, a visit to which is thus described : A long procession of the nuns marched slowly into the chapel and knelt in prayer. Each nun had a crucifix and a string of beads attached, and whatever may have been the case with their thoughts, their eyes never wandered, notwithstanding strangers were gazing at them. Some were young and pretty, others old and plain, but the sacred character of their labor of love invested them all with beauty. We said the eyes of none wandered. Perhaps we ought to confess that the quick, sharp glance of one, apparently younger than the others, stared at us for a moment; but it was only curiosity—womanly curiosity—and what woman has not the curiosity to look at me. Yet that moment was fruitful of thought, and as we saw the sad, dark-eyed beauty rise in her place and mechanically follow her more staid sisters, our mind went back to the days of chivalry, when gallant knights rode with lance at rest, or wielded the heavy battle-axe in heroic deeds that they might win recognition from the proud ladies who looked down upon them. And as we thought, it seemed that the most gallant deeds which men of this nineteenth century might do, would be to rescue young and pretty nuns—who wanted to be rescued—from the silence and sadness of the nunnery.

We are now arrested by an immense structure even larger than the institution just passed; it is the Montreal College, which educates ecclesiastics, and also day pupils, and is under the care of the Sulpician fathers. The two Martello towers in front of the college are relics of the times when incessant strife raged between the settlers and the Indians. Sherbrooke street is adorned with the private residences for which the citizens of Montreal are proud, and in your drive around the town, previous to or after returning from your Park Mountain drive, it will repay one to drive through Sherbrooke, Dennis and Dorchester streets. The McGill College, University and spacious grounds are the next points.

As we pass along Sherbrooke street, in the distance we observe, as we glance up St. Famille street, the enormous Hotel Dieu, with a large, bright dome, a free hospital for all, under Roman Catholic direction.

Returning to the Post Office, preferably by Beaver Hall Hill, we shall not fail to be struck by the number of handsome churches erected there together. On the right is the Unitarian church, on the left, successively a Presbyterian, Baptist, and Jewish synagogue. Near by, on Craig street, is a towered building occupied by the Young Men's Christian Association.

We are soon at the new St. Lawrence Hall, and before mentioning the drives that may be taken outside the city, it may be well to call attention to a few places near at hand a business man or student may be interested in visiting : The Corn Exchange, foot of St. John street, the Merchants' Exchange, St. Sacrament street, the office of the Telegraph Co., and the Open Stock Exchange, St. Francis Xavier street. Near the beginnning of St. James street, on St. Cabriel street, is the Geological Museum, open daily from 10 to 4, containing an admirable collection of North American minerals, and many interesting fossils. Here may be seen what many geologists regard as the most primitive record of life, the *Eoxoon Canaddense*, first noticed at Perth, Ontario, by a Mr. Wilson. From the fact that the oldest fossil bearing stratum, the Laurentian, is the backbone, geographically, of Canada, and because of the great variety of rocks found in the immediate vicinity of Montreal, this museum is particularly attractive to a lover of science. An effort is on foot to deprive the city of this collection, and, for the sake of centralization, remove it to Ottawa. I offer this as an apology in case it should be removed.

DRIVES.

As I have said two or three times, by far the most pleasant drive is up the brow of Mount Royal, called the Park Mountain drive. There are, presumably, two roads : the shorter returns by McTavish street, the other by Bleury. The park was laid out by Mr. Olmstead, the designer of Central Park, New York, whose achievements there were recognized by a statue adorning one of the entrances. The river view from Mount Royal is delightful, and must be seen to be appreciated. I dare not attempt to describe it. A suggestion of how to get a hundred pictures of every conceivable shape or form of landscape views, containing mountain, plain, river, lake, hillside, valley, etc., etc., is to close the eye, place the hands on each end of the forehead, and every time the carriage moves a hundred feet open the eyes, and you have an entire new picture. Keep this up until you have had an elegant sufficiency of view. The next drive is around the mountain, and was the best until the completion of the Park Mountain drive; it is pleasant and attractive, when it includes a drive to the Catholic and Protestant cemeteries, giving a view of the monuments and tombs. The drive to Lachine is next, and is of interest. The drive to Longue Point, along the St. Lawrence in the opposite direction to the last, gives us an entirely different kind of scenery. It takes us through the village of Hochelaga, the terminus of the new railroad, the Quebec, Montreal, Ottawa and Occidental, which runs along the north shore of the St. Lawrence, and develops tracts of country as yet unbenefitted by the iron horse. About a mile from the depot is the beautiful convent of the Sisters of the Holy Names of Jesus and Mary. Many young ladies from the United States have been educated at this convent. The next noteworthy building is the Lunatic Asylum. This immense house, containing nearly 300 maniacs, idiots, and imbeciles, is controlled by the Sisters of Providence ; these ladies, with the exception of six guardians for desperate characters, and a physician, have sole charge. They find no trouble in the care of the numerous inmates, and by their kindness and tact restore mental balance, in all the cases where cure is possible, in a tithe the time it used to take in the old days, when the insane were treated with harshness and cruelty. On our way to Longue Point, the villages of Longueuil, Boucherville and Varennes lie on the opposite bank of the river. The drive to the Back River is an attractive one, and with citizens the most attractive of all ; the beautiful Convent of the Sacred Heart is situated here, and its grounds, finely laid out, lead directly to the water's edge. The bridge which spans the river at this place—a branch of the Ottawa—affords one of the characteristic sights of Canada, the piloting of a raft through a tortuous channel. The size of an ordinary raft, its great value, from $100,000 to $300,000, the excitement of the captain and his French and Indian crew, with the constant perils threatening the whole structure, all conjoin to make up a scene to be dwelt upon and long remembered. Thus hoping the same will be said of your visit to Montreal, I shall advise all to visit

QUEBEC.

Tourists can either take the Grand Trunk, the North Shore, or the Richelieu & Ontario Navigation Co.'s line of steamers. Tickets can be procured of the Company's agent opposite the new St. Lawrence Hall building, where staterooms, etc., may be secured. I assume that the river is the route selected, and that the reader is fairly on his way to that ancient city and former capital. Passing a group of islands below Montreal and the mouth of the Ottawa river, we soon arrive at

SOREL,

forty-five miles below—the first landing made by the steamer. It was built upon the site of a fort built in 1755, by M. De Tracy and was for many years the summer residence of many succesive Governors of Canada. Five miles below, the broad expanse of the river is called

LAKE ST. PETER,

which is about nine miles wide. The St. Francis river enters here. Large rafts are observed here slowly floating to the great mart at Quebec.

THREE RIVERS

is situated at the confluence of the River St. Maurice and St. Lawrence, ninety miles below Montreal, and the same distance above Quebec. It is one of the oldest settled towns in Canada, having been founded in 1618. It is well laid out and contains many good buildings, among which are the Court House, the Jail, the Roman Catholic Church, the Ursuline Convent the English and Wesleyan churches. The population of Three Rivers is about 9,200.

BATISCAN

is situated on the north shore of the river, one-hundred and seventeen miles below Montreal. It is the last place the steamers stop before reaching Quebec. It is a place of little importance.

In passing down the St. Lawrence from Montreal, the country upon its banks presents a sameness in its general scenery, until we approach the vicinity of Quebec. The villages and hamlets are decidedly French in character, generally made up of small buildings, the better class of which are painted white or whitewashed, with red roofs. Prominent in the distance appear the tile-covered spires of the Catholic churches, which are all constructed in that unique style of architecture so peculiar to that church.

During your stay in Quebec stop at the St. Louis Hotel, and if carriages are desired the hotel will furnish the same. This was made necessary in order to stop the imposition that is practiced by outside parties. There are four splendid drives laid out for the visitor and tourist; a neat little pamphlet descriptive of the same, entitled "Views of the City of Quebec," will be given you *free* by asking the clerk, Mr. Phillips, or the news agent, Mr. King, of the St. Louis Hotel.

CITY OF QUEBEC.

Quebec, by its historic fame and its unequaled scenery, is no ordinary or common-place city, for though, like other large communities, it carries on trade, commerce and manufactures; cultivates art, science and literature; abounds in charities, and professes special regard to the amenities of

STOP AT THE

Saint Louis Hotel

QUEBEC

social life, it claims particular attention as being a strikingly unique old place, the stronghold of Canada, and, in fact, the Key of the Province. Viewed from any of its approaches, it impresses the stranger with the conviction of strength and permanency. The reader of American history, on entering its gates or wandering over its squares, ramparts and battle-fields, puts himself at once in communion with the illustrious dead. The achievements of daring mariners, the labors of self-sacrificing Missionaries of the Cross, and the conflicts of military heroes, who bled and died in the assault and defence of its walls, are here re-read with ten-fold interest. Then the lover of nature in her grandest and most rugged, as in her gentler and most smiling forms, will find in and around it an affluence of sublime and beautiful objects. The man of science, too, may be equally gratified, for here the great forces of nature and secret alchemy may be studied with advantage. Quebec can never be a tame or insipid place, and with moderate opportunities for advancement, it must become one of the greatest cities of the New World in respect to learning, art, commerce and manufactures.

The city of Quebec was founded by Samuel de Champlain, in 1608. In 1622 the population was reduced to fifty souls.

In June, 1759, the English army under General Wolfe landed upon the Island of Orleans. On the 12th of September took place the celebrated battle of the Plains of Abraham, which resulted in the death of Wolfe, and the defeat of the French army. A force of 5,000 English troops, under General Murray, were left to garrison the fort. The city is very interesting to a stranger; it is the only walled city in North America.

Cape Diamond, upon which the citadel stands, is three hundred and forty-five feet in height, and derives its name from the quantity of crystal mixed with the granite below its surface. The fortress includes the whole space on the Cape.

Above the spot where General Montgomery was killed is now the inclined place, running to the top of the bank; it is five hundred feet long, and is used by the Government to convey stores and other articles of great weight to the fortress.

THE CITADEL

will, perhaps, prove the point of greatest interest to many, from the historical associations connected therewith, and from the fact that it is considered an impregnable fortress. It covers an enclosed area of forty acres, and is some three hundred and forty feet above the river level. The zigzag passages through which you enter the fortress, between high and massive granite walls, is swept at every turn by formidable batteries of heavy guns. On the forbidding river walls and at each angle or possible commanding point, guns of heavy calibre sweep every avenue of approach by the river. Ditches, breast-works and frowning batteries command the approaches by land from the famed " Plains of Abraham." The precipitous bluffs, rising almost perpendicularly from the river three hundred and forty feet, present a natural barrier which may be swept with murderous fire, and the covered ways of approach and retreat, the various kinds and calibre of guns, mortars, howitzers and munitions of war, will be viewed with eager interest. Among the places of note may be mentioned the Plains of Abraham, with its humble monument, marking the place where fell the illustrious Wolfe; the Governor's Garden, with its monument to Wolfe and Montcalm; the spot where fell the American general, Montgomery; St. John's Gate, the only gate remaining of the five that originally pierced the walls of the city; the Roman Catholic Cathedral, with its many fine old paintings; the Episcopal Cathedral; the Esplanade, from which is one of the finest views in the world; Houses of Parliament; Spencer Wood, the residence of the Lieut. Governor, Laval University, &c., &c.

The city and environs abound in drives, varying from five to thirty miles, in addition to being on the direct line of travel to the far-famed Saguenay, Murray Bay, Kamouraska, Gacouna, Rimouski Gaspe, and other noted watering places.

Quebec can minister abundantly to the tastes of those who like to fish, yacht, or shoot. Yachting, in fact, has become of late the leading recreation in Quebec. You can on those mellow Saturday afternoons of August and September meet the whole sporting and fashionable world of Upper Town on the Durham Terrace or Lower Town wharves, bent on witnessing a trial of speed or seamanship between the *Mouette*, the *Black Hawk*, the *Wasp*, the *Shannon*, the *Bonhomme Richard*, and half a score of crack yachts, with their owners.

Let us see what the city contains :—First, the west wing, built about 1789, by Governor Haldimand, to enlarge the old chateau burnt down in January, 1734; this mouldering pile, now used as the Normal School, is all that remains of the stately edifice of old, overhanging and facing the Cul-de-Sac, where the lordly Count de Frontenac held his quasi regal court in 1691; next, the Laval University, founded in 1854, conferring degrees under its loyal charter; the course of study is similar to that of the celebrated European University of Louvain; then there is the Quebec Seminary, erected by Bishop Laval, at Montmorency, in 1663; the Ursuline Convent, founded in 1636 by Madame de la Peltrie; this nunnery, with the Roman Catholic Cathedral, which was built in 1646, contains many valuable paintings, which left France about 1789; the General Hospital, founded two centuries ago by Monseigneur de St. Vallier; in 1759, it was the chief hospital for the wounded and the dying of the memorable battle of the 13th September; Arnold and his Continentals found protection against the rigors of a Canadian winter behind its walls in 1775-6; the Hotel Dieu Nunnery, close to Palace Gate, dating more than 200 years back.

As to the views to be obtained from Durham Terrace, the Glacis and the Citadel, they are unique in grandeur. Each street has its own familiar vista of the surrounding country.

THE SHRINE AND FALLS OF STE. ANNE.

At the distance of about twenty miles below Quebec is the village of Ste. Anne de Beaupre, sometimes called Ste. Anne du Nord, and always called *La Bonne Ste. Anne*, to whom is consecrated the parish church, erected about four years ago by the Pope into a shrine of the first order, in which is a fine painting by the famous artist LeBrun, Ste. Anne and the Virgin, presented by M. de Tracy, Viceroy of New France, in 1666, to the church, for benefits received. The festival day of this Saint is the 26th of July, at which time thousands of pilgrims proceed not only by steamer and carriage, but on foot, to this holy shrine; many walk the whole distance from Quebec to the church as a penance, or in performance of vows. The church is a new building, the old one having been found too small for the accommodation of the crowds of pilgrims who resorted there. In it are placed thousands of crutches, left by those who departed after being cured of the lameness and other maladies by the Bonne Ste. Anne, whose praises are world wide, for hither congregate daily thousands of pilgrims from all parts to be cured of their infirmities. Deposited in the sanctuary is a holy relic, being a finger bone of the saint herself, on kissing which the devotee is immediately relieved of all worldly ills and misfortunes. Wonder begins and misbelief vanishes on gazing at the piles of crutches; there one beholds unmistakable evidence of the unlimited medicinal power of the mother of the Virgin. Daily are the proofs of this power; the stranger can see with his own eyes the decrepid, the halt, the sore, the lame, the wounded carried into the holy sanctuary and depart therefrom, after kissing the holy relict, cured and whole. Many are the scenes here witnessed of the despairing filled with renewed hope, and the feeble and faint glad again with strength and health. Countless are the anecdotes of the hopelessly blind and lame returning to their friends with sight and firm limbs, leaving behind them their bandages and crutches. Incredulity vanishes before such evidence, and the sceptic leaves the shrine of Ste. Anne with convictions deeply settled in his soul. Within three miles of the village are the Falls of Ste. Anne, which consists of seven cascades, one of which rushes through a narrow chasm, which can be leaped by one of strong nerves and sinews, but powerful as Ste. Anne is, and devoted as she is to miracles, it is doubtful whether even she could save the unfortunate who misses his leap.

The fishing above and below the Falls is very good for both salmon and trout, and the scenery of that wild description generally characteristic of the Laurentian ranges.

MONTMORENCY FALLS

is seven miles below Quebec. The road is very pleasant, passing through the French village of Beauport. Those who expect to see a second Niagara will be very much disappointed. The steam descends in silvery threads, over a precipice 240 feet in height, and, in connection with the surrounding scenery, is extremely picturesque and beautiful, but inspires none of the awe felt at Niagara.

POINT LEVIS,

on the other side of the river opposite Quebec, will interest the stranger very much, immense and stupendous fortifications being in process of erection. Most tourists visiting Quebec, pay the Saguenay a visit. The ticket office of this line is opposite the St. Louis Hotel, where my genial friend, Mr. R. M. Stocking, will cheerfully impart any information required, he being the agent for all railroads and steamboats in Canada or that connect with the same in the United States.

WE CALL THEM TRAMPS.

During the Centennial year many foreigners were always found among the list of passengers from every country. The proverbial English tourist cannot be mistaken by any but this year, 1876, we had many who were too green or unsophistical to be in that class. Now this truthful occurrence which I am about to relate is original and occurred upon one of the Richelieu & Ontario Navigation Company's line of boats. The Englisman was relating to his newly found friend his opinion of the United States, etc., in his own peculiar style. Hi don't like this blarsted country you know! Why, said his friend, what fault can you find with America? Oh! Hi've been all over it you know, and can't find any sawciety there. Society, said his friend, what do you mean by society? Oh, dear me, you have no gentlemen or gentlemen's sons in h'America Why, what do you mean by gentlemen and gentlemen's sons? Oh! Hi mean gentlemen who never did any work you know, nor their sons either. You make a mistake there, my worthy friend, we have millions of them here but we call them tramps, and I have often thought it the best definition to a tramp I ever heard, for if there are gentlemen and their sons here who never did any work they will soon make good timber for tramps if they are not already.

RIVER SAGUENAY.

To the pleasure-seeker, or to the man of science, there can be nothing more refreshing and delightful, anything affording more food for reflection or scientific observation, than a trip to that most wonderful of rivers, the Saguenay. On the way thither, the scenery of the Lower St. Lawrence is extraordinarily picturesque; a broad expanse of water, interspersed with rugged solitary islets, highly cultivated islands, and islands covered with trees to the water's edge, hemmed in by lofty and precipitous mountains on the one side, and by a continuous street of houses, relieved by beautifully situated villages, the spires of whose tin-covered churches glitter in the sunshine, affords a prospect so enchanting, that, were nothing else to be seen, the tourist would be well repaid; but when, in addition to all this, the tourist suddenly passes from a landscape unsurpassed for beauty into a region of primitive grandeur, where art has done nothing, and nature everything; when, at a single bound, civilization is left behind and nature stares him in the face, in naked majesty; when he sees Alps on Alps arise; when he floats over unfathomable depths, through a mountain gorge, the sublime entirely overwhelms the sense of sight and fascinates imagination.

The change produced upon the thinking part of man, in passing from the broad St. Lawrence into the seemingly narrow and awfully deep Saguenay, whose waters leave the sides of the towering mountains, which almost shut out the very light of heaven, is such as no pen can paint nor tongue describe. It is a river one should see if only to know what dreadful aspects nature can assume in wild moods. Compared to it the Dead Sea is blooming, and the wildest ravines cosy and smiling; it is wild and grand, apparently, in spite of itself. On either side rise cliffs varying in perpendicular height from 1,200 to 1,600 feet, and this is the character of the River Saguenay from its mouth to its source. Ha! Ha! bay, which is 60 miles from its mouth, affords the first landing and anchorage. The name of this bay is said to arise from the circumstance of early navigators proceeding in sailing vessels up a river of this kind for 60 miles, with eternal sameness of feature, stern and high rocks on which they could not land, and no bottom for their anchors, at last broke out into laughing Ha! Ha! when they found landing and anchorage. This wonderful river seems one huge mountain rent asunder at some remote age by some great convulsion of nature. The reader who goes to see it (and all ought to do so who can, for it is one of the great natural wonders of the continent), can add to the poetical filling up of the picture from his own imagination.

This beautiful trip is easy and facile of accomplishment, as new and magnificent boats, rivaling in luxuriousness with any in our island waters, run regularly to Ha! Ha! bay, on board of which the pleasure seeker will experience all that comfort and accommodation which is necessary to the full enjoyment of such a trip.

To the foregoing descriptions we append an extract from the letter of a writer in the Buffalo *Commercial Advertiser*, who has apparently gone over the "ground" with much satisfaction. Speaking of the great pleasure route, he says:

"There is probably no route in the known world presenting more attractions to the tourist than that from Buffalo to Montreal and Quebec, via. Lake Ontario and the St. Lawrence river; presenting, first, the visit to the great cataract, next, Lake Ontario, the river St. Lawrence, and the romantic scenery of the 'Thousand Isles'; then the sublime rapids, increasing in grandeur to the great culmination of the ' Lachine rapids,' and finally finishing with the beautiful scenery of and around the Falls of Montmorency, at Quebec, and down the Saguenay—all combine to make up more of the wild, romantic and sublime than can be found in the same number of miles and almost any traveled route in the known world."

Returning to Montreal for our trip down Lake Champlain and Lake George, to Saratoga, Albany, New York and Boston, as most of the tourists have tickets for these destinations, the routes need only be mentioned. The Delaware & Hudson Canal Company Railroad, and Central Vermont have ticket offices in Montreal, where information is courteously dispensed by obliging, gentlemanly clerks at all times. It would be useless here to print the time tables of the different roads, as changes occur too often for such information to be reliable. As your are supposed to be quartered at the new St. Lawrence Hall, which is in the heart of the city, and contains the Grand Trunk Railroad and Delaware & Hudson Canal Company Offices, and directly opposite is the Central Vermont office, presided over by A. C. Stonegrave, any time-table required is easily obtainable; also adjoining is the office of the Richelieu and Ontario Navigation Company.

All railroads issuing summer excursion tickets through, over this line, allow passengers, if they desire, to procure at Port Kent depot a ticket which entitles them to visit Au Sable Chasm, and to return to Port Kent for 75 cents.

Leaving Montreal in the morning, by taking the first train on the Delaware & Hudson Canal Railroad, if you wish to make Lake George, Saratoga or Albany the same day, your ticket may read Lake Champlain Co. steamers, but it is all the same—boat and rail belong to the same parties. Should you desire to take Lake Champlain, leave Montreal in the afternoon and go to Au Sable Chasm, via Port Kent, remain over night at Lake View House, taking the boat at 8 A. M. from there to Fort Ticonderoga, and then down Lake George, or proceed on the train at 10:30. By getting off at Port Kent the distance to Lake View House is only three miles by stage over a first-class plank road ; therefore, it may be said, if you desire to make both lakes on the same day, you are compelled to leave Montreal in the afternoon and go to Au Sable Chasm via Port Kent, and remain over night at the Lake View Hotel, which will be found to be an excellent house ; taking the boat in the morning. If tickets read by the Central Vermont Railroad you go to Burlington, where you arrive for supper, and as the boat does not leave there until nine o'clock in the morning, you have plenty of time to see that beautiful city before the leaving of the boat ; at any rate you won't have to rise as early as if you were at Plattsburg.

MY FIRST VISIT TO AU SABLE CHASM.

As long as anything shall remain green in my memory, I feel confident it will be the impression of that charming view and grand natural spectacle, Au Sable Chasm.

Arising early in the morning, if not with the lark, a very good second in the race, I was invited by the manager of the Lake View House to visit the chasm. Accepting the same, we proceeded through the gate and down the steps, which I did not stop to count ; but the number was suffi-

presumed you get there. Lake George Junction is where you change cars and connect for Baldwin, which is a ride of about fifteen minutes. You are now supposed to have arrived on board the company's steamers *Horicon* or *Ticonderoga* and are sailing up Lake George. Now, if the reader expects me to describe Lake George, I shall simply say No ! with a large N. It is too much ; its praises have been written and sung for the past half century by thousands. I shall with pleasure and relief to myself ask the loan of your scissors. Thanks; now we can comply with your wishes : We have started on our trip through this magical lake. It is difficult to describe the quiet delight one feels as he gazes on the expanse of the tranquil azure spread before him like a part of the sky inlaid on the emerald bosom of the earth. Peace is in the very air which lazily slumbers over the water, while the monotone of the silvery ripples rolling on the yellow sands, and the musical moan of the breeze in the cone-scented pines, seem to carry the soul back to other days. Lake George is, indeed, like a work of art of the highest order, for it has the quality of improving, the more one studies its attractions, and the ever-harmonious flow of lines constantly suggests a composition of consumate genius in which every effect has been combined to produce a certain ideal.

Now, dear reader, I have a favor to ask of you ; read this little book as far as Saratoga description commences; then lay it aside, and feast the eyes on Lake George for the next two hours, and, if you can describe its beauties, do so to the best of your ability, and forward to me, 21 Chestnut Park, Rochester, N. Y., and it shall have a place in this work, and you shall have the credit for the same ;—the task was too much for me.

CAMPING OUT.

The lake is a famous camping-ground, during July and August, and its enjoyments, with bits of sound advice, cannot be better given than by the following, from Stoddart's charming guide to Lake George :

"'The lovely islands are suddenly astir with busy throngs. Rocks are decked with blue and gray, the tree tops blush with bunting ; shores put on a flannelly hue, and shadowy point blossom out in duck and dimity. It is safe to say that in the course of the season a thousand people taste the pleasures and overcome the difficulties that but season the glorious dish of camp life at Lake George. Among the necessaries are a light axe, long handle frying-pan, tin pail for water or coffee, tin plate, pint cup, knife and fork, and fishing tackle. A stove-top laid on a fire-place of stones and mud, and supplied with one length of stove-pipe, is a positive luxury to the cook. Spruce boughs for a bed, with two or three good woolen blankets for covering, will be found very comfortable ; a small bag to fill with leaves or moss for a pillow pays for itself in one night. Flannel or woolen clothing, with roomy boots and a soft felt hat, is ordinarily the safest dress. Ladies, wear what you have a mind to—you will, anyway—but let it be flannel next to you, good strong shoes underfoot, and a man's felt hat overhead ; take the man along too—he will be useful to take the fish off your hook, run errands, etc.

Boats and provisions may be obtained at almost any of the hotels. Bacon, salt pork, bread and butter, Boston crackers, tea, coffee, sugar, pepper and salt, with a tin box or two for containing the same, are among the things need-

genial in its bright skies and pure, fresh atmosphere. Conventionalities that obtain at other resorts are not held here, and it is possible for gentlemen to wear blue shirts and soft hats, and for ladies to travel without male escort other than the necessary compliment of guides to furnish motive power, from one end of the wilderness to the other.

Full dress is seldom seen, even at the most fashionable resorts, and is exceeded in absurdity only by the conventional "stage trapper," who occasionally burst upon the astonished wilderness in fringed buckskin. Your right to enter the best society will not be questioned because of dress. Clothing ordinarily worn is sufficent for all occasions here."

The Adirondack region is steadily growing in favor as a resort for persons afflicted with throat and lung troubles; and while it is not by any means a sure cure for *all*, however deeply seated the disease may have become, yet if persons so afflicted will go there in time, they will find the dry, pure air, impregnated as it is with balsam and pine, to be of infinite relief, and many living witnesses are there found to prove its benefits. Several articles have been written upon this subject which misled the public, and, in consequence, many people, past all possible cure, have been sent there, with only natural results. We would only say, consult your physician, and, if you are not past cure, we believe this section to be as nearly affording a remedy as any spot on the continent.

Places of entertainment, from the well-appointed hotel on the border to the rude log-house and open camp of the interior, are found at short intervals throughout the entire wilderness, all waiting with open doors to receive the stranger.

Guides and boats may be had at all the hotels.

Under head of "Gateways" will be found the nearest points reached by railroad and stage routes, distances, etc., to the most prominent resorts.

GATEWAYS.

PORT KENT

is the station on the Delaware & Hudson Canal Company's Railroad on through route, New York to Canada, all parties who desire to visit Au Sable Chasm, three miles by good plank road, and Lake View House, stop off.

THE BEST point for entrance into or exit from the Adirondacks. Stages run to all points from Au Sable Chasm to Au Sable Station and Forks, etc., etc.

From Plattsburg, take Chateaugay Railroad, thirty-six miles to Lyon Mountain, thence by stage four miles to Ralph's, on upper Chateaugay Lake.

From Au Sable (20 miles west of Plattsburg on branch railroad). Stages leave here every morning (Sundays excepted) on arrival of early trains, for French's, 18 miles; Franklin Falls, 20 miles; Bloomingdale, 28 miles; Loon Lake House, on Loon Lake, 28 miles; Rainbow House, on Rainbow Lake, 35 miles; Martin's on Saranac Lake, 37 miles; Paul Smith's, on St. Regis Lake, 38 miles; Prospect House, on Saranac Lake, 41 miles; Bartlett's, on Saranac Lake, 49 miles.

From Elizabethtown delightful trips are made into the mountain region, through Keene Valley via. Indian Pass,

THE SAGAMORE,
ON GREEN ISLAND, LAKE GEORGE.

Connected with the main land by bridge.   Added this year

Two Queen Ann Cottages,
  Fifty Rooms for Guests,
    Magnificent Extra Dining Room,

MUSIC HALL AND BALL ROOM.

THIS SPLENDID NEW HOTEL IS OPEN FOR GUESTS FROM

JUNE 10 UNTIL OCTOBER 1ST

IT IS SUPPLIED WITH

Passenger Elevator, Electric Lights and Bells in every Room, as well as other Modern Conveniences.

Its Location the Finest on the Lake.

THE TABLE IS EXCELLENT,
  THE SERVICE UNSURPASSED.

Easy of access by Boats from the North or South, Baldwin or Caldwell, where trains with Palace Cars arrive from Saratoga, New York and intermediate points several times daily.

For Descriptive Circulars and Plan of Rooms, Address

M. O. BROWN,
Lessee and Proprietor,
Bolton Landing, Lake George, Warren Co., N. Y.

and to Au Sable Pond, one of the most beautiful spots in the wilderness, also by North Elba, Lake Placid and Wilmington Notch, passing immediately under the shadow of Whiteface and Haystock Mountains, and out at Au Sable station, or return to Elizabethtown.

FACILITIES FOR LAKE TRAVEL.

The Champlain Transportation Company run a regular line of steamboats the entire length of the lake, making three round trips daily (except Sundays), and stopping at all way landings. The *Horicon* of this line, making the regular connections with the railroad, is a fine side-wheel steamer 203 feet long and 52 feet wide over all, and is 643 tons burden, and will accommodate comfortably 1,000 people. I can truthfully say that upon no inland lake in the world is the passenger service so promptly and regularly done, and passengers so elegantly cared for as upon Lake George.

Caldwell is the railroad terminus, and is the largest town on the lake. It is situated at the extreme southern end, or head of the lake (the waters flowing north and emptying into Lake Champlain, immediately at the ruins of old Fort Ticonderoga). At Caldwell, is located the handsome dock and depot building of the railroad company, whose trains run down the dock immediately to the steamers—one of which leaves upon the arrival of each train for all points down the lake. The railroad was extended to this point in 1883, thus saving at least one hour of time and better facilities for the accommodation of tourists and pleasure travel.

LAKE GEORGE.

Every American, or tourist, should see it at least once. It is the largest of the Adirondack chain, 346 feet above the sea, and 247 above Champlain, 35 miles long and from two to four in width, and fed from mountain brooks and springs coming up from the bottom, making it transparent. It is beautifully dotted with over 200 islands, and surrounded by high mountains, some rising 2,000 feet above the water, clothed with foliage and dotted with villas and picturesque camps; one feels like leaving the boat and remaining in this bower of enchantment. The steamers touch at all points of note and arrive at the Sagamore Hotel, where you can, if you desire, remain over.

CONVENIENCES.

The proprietor, Mr. M. O. Brown, long and popularly known as a hotel man on the lake, will spare no pains to make your sojourn attractive in all respects.

The Hotel is elegantly furnished throughout, has a fast running elevator, and is lighted by the Edison incandescent electric light in every room. Fifty rooms added this year, a new extra dining room, music hall, and ball room. It is supplied with pure water from a Mountain spring.

The Cuisine is perfect. The *Chef* and assistants are from the leading New York Hotels. The Head Waiter, Mr. J. T. McGovern, with his excellent and full corps of carefully trained and experienced waiters, the best that could be obtained. This is the only hotel on the entire lake that employs white male waiters.

In the main office is the Telegraph Office and all requisites needed for comfort.

The Lake steamboats land at the dock directly in front of "The Sagmore." A large number of steam and sailing yachts, and a flotilla of smaller boats are provided for the use of guests to order.

The Livery Stables attached keep constantly on hand saddle horses, buggies, buck-boards, phætons and other carriages of all descriptions, to be had by applying at the office.

The Lake steamboats, HORICON and TICONDEROGA, arrive every morning bringing passengers from Montreal, Lake Champlain and Whitehall, direct to the wharf of the Sagamore where courteous attendants will always be in readiness to assist and serve the guests of this House.

As I have cheerfully recommended tourists for the last three years to make a short stay at least at this delightful resort, the Sagamore, and never met one afterwards who did not thank me for the suggestion; I say to you remain over. I am confident you will never regret it. Connections are, however, arranged for, and you can, if you wish, leave immediately for Caldwell or

SARATOGA SPRINGS,

the focus to which the fashionable world of the United States, indeed, of Europe, is annually drawn. Here are intellectual men, stylish men, the beaux of Society, and the man of the world; ladies of social rank, the managing mother, the marriageable daughters, the fluttering bee of

WHEN YOU VISIT

SARATOGA

—STOP AT—

"THE ADELPHI"

—ENLARGED AND NEWLY FURNISHED FOR—

THE SEASON OF 1886.

W. H. McCAFFERY, PROP'R.

fashion, and the more gentle bird of beauty, are found amidst the throng, for Saratoga is cosmopolitan. As a gentleman said to me one day, "I can meet more of my friends in one hour during the season at Saratoga than I could at home in a week." The ladies here have ample opportunities to display their peculiar charms and graces. The sporting gentleman can also find an opportunity to gratify his peculiar tastes; the philosopher may study human nature; the invalid find perfect health; in fact every one at Saratoga finds that peculiar pleasure they most desire. Of all the elegant hotels which here abound we have not space to mention. I will, therefore, speak of those I know, the United States and Adelphi, confident they can please any one paying them a visit.

The Adelphi Hotel—This new, comfortable and petite hotel is located on Broadway, contains one hundred rooms, is convenient to the springs, etc., etc. Its piazza is elevated one story above the street and commands a splendid view up and down Broadway, as well as Phila street opposite. The proprietor, Mr. Wm. H. McCaffery, is too well known to the traveling community to need one word from me, and the gentlemen connected with the office and other departments of the house, are too well qualified by being the choice of the proprietor, to need commendation. It is "my home" when in Saratoga; that is all I have to say against it. It is the universal opinion of tourists, that no watering place on the continent, of like size, can compare with the unwearying charms of Saratoga. The hotel arrivals some days are upwards of one thousand. One might become almost tired of the world and vote every other place a bore,

CONGRESS SPRING.

—THE—

STANDARD MINERAL WATER.

CATHARTIC, ALTERATIVE, a Specific for disorders of the STOMACH, LIVER and KIDNEYS, ECZEMA, MALARIA, and all IMPURITIES of the BLOOD.

So enviable a name has this famous Mineral Water that the managers of inferior Mineral Springs, desirous of imitating the natural purity of the bottled water of Congress Spring, inject a powerful acid in their bottled water to preserve the crude ingredients in solution—being so heavily laden with

LIME AND IRON DEPOSIT.

With such contrivances, bogus testimonials and doctored analysis cards, they seek to rival the pure Medicinal Water of Congress Spring.

The regular season visitors to Saratoga fully understand these crude, harsh waters, many of them after painful experiences. **In proof of this we can Produce a GREAT MANY RESPONSIBLE NAMES.** But the Saratoga visitors without experience, and many who use the bottled waters (often labeled as curatives for disorders which they positively agravate), should remember that crude, harsh Mineral Waters produce headache, a sense of burning and internal irritation, and do irreparable injury to the digestive organs and kidneys.

CONGRESS WATER,

PURE, NATURAL AND RELIABLE,

NONE GENUINE SOLD ON DRAUGHT.

For Sale by Druggists, Grocers, Wine Merchants and Hotels.

BOTTLE "C" MARK.

Ask for Congress Water and insist on having **NO OTHER.**

but Saratoga scenery, Saratoga atmosphere and Saratoga life would still charm by its ever pleasing peculiarities. Mount McGregor, the place selected above all others for its pure air, etc., etc., as a residence for our hero, Gen. U. S. Grant, who arrived at Saratoga on June 16th, 1885, (during my stay for health), so I had the pleasure of seeing the old veteran while he was being conveyed to the Mount McGregor R. R., which ascends to the top of the mountain, where visitors can go almost every hour and get a view that will well repay them. I left Saratoga on the morning of the 19th of June, and was informed by the conductor of the Mt. McGregor R. R. that General Grant rested well the previous night and slept ten hours. As all are aware our Hero departed this life July 23d, the cottage, however, is kept in the same manner as the day he left it and will become an historic place for visitors who come to Saratoga from all parts of the world.

It is a fact and worthy of note here, that for the past four years there has not been one day during the months of July or August, but they have had a heavy frost on Mount McGregor. I can vouch for the truthfulness of this item because I know him. He is the conductor of the train on the Mt. McGregor R. R., weighs 280 pounds and his name is Frost. (He is a broad-gauge conductor on a narrow-gauge railroad.)

Saratoga contains 10,000 inhabitants, and in the summer season every private house is turned into a boarding house of one or the other class, and therefore boarding houses abound—no space to mention all of them here.

Next in order comes the Springs. First in the list is the old and ever popular Congress Springs.

CONGRESS SPRINGS

was discovered nearly a century ago—1792—by Hon. James Taylor, member of Congress from New Hampshire. The park connected with the Springs is beautifully laid out with walks, groves, flowers, trees, and ponds in which speckled trout abound, fountains, statuary, live deer, etc., etc.; where night and day the beauty and fashion come for pleasure and to imbibe the water of Columbia and Congress Springs, which are within the enclosure. Those who are posted come here and drink, thus avoiding those waters of other springs which are irritating in their nature, and harsh and inflammable to the stomach, injuring the kidneys and producing results irreparable. Read Congress Springs book for 1886.

HATHORN SPRINGS

was accidentally discovered in 1869, and is named after the Hon. H. H. Hathorn, its owner. It is a powerful cathartic. The water is bottled for sale, and is probably the most solid water known, as it is said to contain eight hundred and eighty-eight grains solid contents to a gallon.

EXCELSIOR SPRINGS AND PARK,

some distance from town, as well as others I shall mention you can visit when you take a drive. Washington Spring is on the grounds of one of the hotels. Crystal Pavilion, High Rock, Star, Seltzer, Red, a Spring, Geyser or spouting spring, Robert Ellis, The Vichy, "The Champion Spouting Spring," Hamilton, Putnam, Flat Rock, Magnetic, Sulphur, Iron and Diamond, as well as a number of others which have just been discovered, or may have been before this reaches you. If, however, you are not satisfied with the springs herein mentioned, all I ask is for you to visit the ones mentioned as I did, and accept the cordial invitation of each to take a glass, and if you do not feel the next day that there are springs enough at Saratoga, your feelings will be different from the sensation felt by the writer of this article by a large majority. The drives in this vicinity are numerous. The road to the cemetery (which, I am informed, by one of the oldest inhabitants, in order to start, they were obliged to borrow a corpse from an adjoining county, and now a select few who wish to die happy come and are decently interred,) has been improved, so that the drive there is very much enhanced thereby. By far the prettiest drive, however, is through Broadway from Highland Hill for two miles to Glen Mitchell. The most fashionable drive is that to the lake. Immense sums of money have been expended to widen and beautify this drive, which is 100 feet wide and shaded with trees, and is sprinkled to lay the dust. Visitors pass up on one side and down the other. Saratoga Lake is eight miles long and two and one-half wide. On an eminence on the western shore is Moon's Lake House, proverbial for its sumptuous game suppers. Parties fond of fishing or boating can enjoy this favorite pastime to their full extent. Its fitness for acquatic ,sports has been verified by the many events of that nature which have taken place on its placid waters since 1871, when the Ward brothers vanquished two English crews selected from the best professional oarsmen of Great Britain. Racing is the turf event of the year, and cannot be described here, only mentioned.

Life at Saratoga is two-fold—Home and Hotel. The former is enjoyed by its citizens, who possess some of the most luxurious, refined and elegant houses to be found in the United States. Hotel or fashsionable life is ephemeral in its nature, and, like the beautiful butterfly, its duration is short. In these few brief months wealth, beauty, fashion, and other ingredients not so desirable, intermingle, and amid the gay whirl and excitement of the ball-room at night one is in a constant ecstacy. From his visit to the springs in the morning, promenades or drives in the afternoon, the music, lawn sociable and glittering fireworks at night, one wonders what time there is for even nature's balmy, sweet restorer—sleep. Anticipating your stay at Saratoga to have come to an end, you can depart for Albany any morning via Delaware and Hudson Canal Co.'s R. R., or West Shore R. R., who run solid trains to and from Saratoga to New York, and New York to Saratoga, Pullman Buffett cars. Some having tickets to New York by rail or boat, and desire to visit Boston, I advise everyone to take the Fall River Line to Boston. If you have tickets to Boston via Albany take the Boston and Albany Railroad, which is first-class.

NEW YORK.

To those visiting New York for the first time, a few words of advice may not come amiss. I therefore suggest arriving, if possible, by daylight. Everyone in the city minds their own business—a credit in some ways ; but some people make it their business to fleece the stranger. I would therefore say, keep your own council. If information be required ask a policeman. Upon arrival, take cars or stage, if possible, to destination. If you desire any of the hotels represented in this work, you will always find one or more trusty porters at trains or boats. Avoid, if possible, the hacks, unless you make a fair, square bargain before entering the vehicle ; your trunk or valise may accompany you with carriage. You will always find upon all trains or boats, courteous agents of the different baggage and express companies, who will take your check, giving a receipt for the same, which relieves you and saves much trouble and annoyance, as their delivery system is prompt and their charges a stipulated price ; no deviation, except for quantity.

Something should be said here regarding the metropolis of the American Continent, but space as well as time prevents. As everything seen here is in grandeur superior to elsewhere, the impression made upon the mind while here will be everlasting, I shall not try to befog the mind with as meager a mention as I am capable of giving, but simply

IMPORTANT.—Travelers arriving at or leaving Grand Central Depot, New York City, for business, pleasure, or to visit summer resorts, will find superior accommodations at this Hotel. European plan. 600 elegant rooms at $1 and upwards, per day. Restaurant, Cafe and Wine Rooms supplied with the best, at moderate prices. Guests save carriage hire, and by handing their Baggage Checks to Hotel Clerk can have Baggage delivered to and from this depot in 15 minutes, free of charge.

GRAND UNION HOTEL, Opposite Grand Central Depot, New York City.

4th AVENUE, 41st and 42d STS.   W. D. GARRISON, Manager.

mention the principal hotels. The first one at hand is the Grand Union Hotel, 42d street near the Grand Central Depot. Money-getting being the chief aim of life, its proper expenditure should not prove of secondary importance. That travel consumes a much larger portion of our finances than it should, is evident from the fact that but few possess the scret of retrenching in that direction. Two important factors of expense in travel is carriage hire and transfer of baggage, and that the traveling public is more generally becoming disposed to throw off their former burden, is patent from the army of guests who daily register at and fill the 600 rooms (reduced to $1.00 and upwards per day), at the Grand Union Hotel, opposite the Grand Central Depot, New York City. Its European plan, elegant restaurants, café, lunch and wine rooms, unexcelled cuisine, moderate prices, courteous treatment, unchallenged management, coupled with its guests incurring no expense for carriage hire, or baggage transfer, with elevated railway, horse cars and stages to all parts of the city passing its doors, renders the Grand Union one of the most desirable of homes for travelers in the city, and also established its success and world-famed popularity.

MURRAY HILL HOTEL

Park Avenue, Fortieth and Forty-first Streets,

One Block from the GRAND CENTRAL DEPOT.

The only First-class Hotel in New York City, on both American and European plans. It occupies the highest ground, and is the HEALTHIEST OF LOCATIONS. For Transient Guests, Tourists, Travelers, or as a residence for families, none more cool, healthful or pleasant can be found.

N. B.—Guests of the Murray Hill Hotel have their baggage transferred to and from the Grand Central Depot free of charge.

A MAGNIFICENT HOTEL.

The Murray Hill Hotel is situated on Park Avenue, in New York City, but one block from the Grand Central Depot. A more convenient hotel site for the accommodation of the newly arrived traveler who would at the earliest moment find a home could not have been selected. The house stands upon the highest grade in New York, and, of course occupies the healthiest of locations. It is of great size, extending two hundred feet on the Avenue, more than two hundred feet on Fortieth street on the one side, and on Forty-first street on the other. It is of granite, brown stone and brick, fire-proof. When the traveler finds a hotel in every way meeting his demands for comfort, he may honestly praise it while he disparages no other. For New York contains many costly structures, whose proprietors severally believe that their guests have reason to be satisfied. Hotels are not advertised as second-class by those that manage them. The man who is used to comfort at home is perhaps as good a judge as any one concerning what constitutes a satisfactory hotel. But, if you come to New York in the summer, I recommend you to this house, for in all this city there can be no healthier place in the warm season. There is a satisfaction felt at once upon entrance to this beautiful house. The vestibule is apparently just large enough, the handsome, short flight of marble steps that lead to the office seems to be just long enough, the great hall seems just high enough to satisfy fully the idea that one has of proper architectural proportion. The floor is of marble, but not the hideous black and white inset diagonal. The Sienna is set against the slate and is a carpet pattern. One rather expects it to be soft and yielding to the foot, it looks so like a Wilton. The office is roomy; not three or four only, but forty people may range themselves along its handsome counter ready to sign, in regular order, the register. The book stand is no contracted affair, but space enough is given to allow display of, and easy access to, all periodicals and newspapers. Everything is on a grand scale, but altogether convenient. The great fire-place, which, with its huge burning logs, in winter invites the guest to share its comfort, is an attraction that merits and receives enthusiastic comment. The electric clock, lighted at night, the chandeliers which at the proper time, because of the light touch of a knob somewhere, instantly illuminate halls and parlors, have their supply of electricity from the great machines in the basement, and the ice that is used for any purpose through all the house is made in huge condensers there. All the departments seem to be at all times in the best working order. All the employés seem ever willing to do their best to please the guest. There is a painstaking to furnish information when it is asked; if one clerk does not know he directs you to one who does. In the matter of meals, they are ready at all hours. At the time of registry, the choice is made between the American or the European plan, but the restaurants above and below stairs are always available. It would be easy for me to compliment the management and the efficient office staff, but that goes for the saying. As space is limited, I need only advise you to give the Murray Hill Hotel your patronage once; they will see that you make it your home thereafter.

THE GRAND CENTRAL HOTEL
667 TO 677 BROADWAY.

American Plan, full board, $2.50. $3.00 and $3.50 per day. Rooms on European Plan, $1 per day and upwards. Special rates for families and permanent guests.

This Hotel is within one block of four lines of Street and Elevated Railroads. The new Broadway Surface Railroad passes the door, connecting with all lines of railroad and boats, affording rapid communication with business centres and places of amusement, and is justly regarded the best Hotel in the city.

ATTRACTIONS OF THE GRAND CENTRAL HOTEL.

This Hotel is universally acknowledged the coolest in New York. The wide straight halls running from Broadway to Mercer street, insure perfect circulation of air. The five large and elegant parlors. The handsomely decorated and cheerful Dining and Supper Rooms. It is provided with two of Otis & Co.'s celebrated Elevators. Six outside Fire Escapes have been recently added, which, with five wide stairways, from roof to ground floor makes the "GRAND CENTRAL HOTEL"

THE SAFEST HOTEL IN AMERICA.

Each floor in the building is nightly patrolled by a Watchman with a tell-tale Clock.

FAYMAN & SPRAGUE, Proprietors.

The next on the list is the Grand Central Hotel, Broadway, one of the largest in the city. It has lately been refitted, re-decorated and re-furnished, and under its present proprietors, Messrs. Fayman & Sprague, is receiving the patronage its merits deserve. It is run on the American and European plans, so that anyone can be pleased. Its graded prices, its location and appointments, together with the friends one meets here, as it is patronized by more Southerners than any hotel in New York, makes it a pleasant place for tourist or traveler. I make it my home when in the city, and feel confident you will be pleased and recommend your friends there after a visit, the same as I do you. There was some talk of changing the name of this "landmark," on account of the thorough change in the hotel and management, although I confess it would be applicable to the situation, as everything else has been changed; it would be better for its patrons to advertise the changes than the new name. Therefore, no matter what they call the Grand Central, it will please you as a hotel, and its prices are not extravagant.

While in New York, about the middle of June, I thought it would be a good idea if some one of the many merchants in the city were to advertise in this little volume; knowing it is not thrown away but retained as a souvenir, it will be a perpetual advertisement; therefore I induced Ehrich Brothers, 8th avenue, 24th and 25th streets, to take a page, and after visiting the many departments and seeing articles useful and ornamental for male and female, to wear or use, every day in life from the cradle to the grave, from a needle to an anchor, at prices so low were it at my home I could

LE PAGE'S LIQUID GLUE is used by Pullman Palace Car Co., Mason & Hamlin Organ and Piano Co., and by thousands of first class manufacturers and mechanics throughout the world for all kinds of fine work. Pronounced STRONGEST ADHESIVE KNOWN. Sold in tin cans for mechanics and amateurs, and in bottles for family use. The total quantity sold between January, 1880, and January, 1885, in all parts of the world amounted to over 32 MILLION BOTTLES.

never get away from their stores with a cent in my pocket;
therefore, I say, do not carry too much money along with
you unless you take the precaution to have a dray or express
wagon to remove the goods. Space would not permit
mentioning articles desired, and would therefore invite
tourists and others to visit their stores, and inspect all departments.
I would like to say here that I published this
book and advised the advertisers therein to take the space,
feeling it would bring back to them four-fold what they paid
me. It will, therefore, afford me pleasure to have you
mention to any of the advertisers that it was through my
solicitation and this work that you favored them with your
patronage; it will do you no harm and benefit me.

BOSTON

is one of the most interesting of American cities, not only
on account of its thrilling traditions and historical associations,
but for public enterprise and social culture, educational
and literary facilities. Boston is peculiarly Boston,
and no one can describe its public, private or natural beauties
in the space allotted me here. The principal sights are
Bunker Hill Monument, Faneuil Hall, the Common, Public
Garden, Old and New State houses, Public Library, Old and
New South Churches, Natural History buildings, Agricultural
building, Institute of Technology, New Trinity Church,
Mount Auburn, Harvard University building, Music Hall,
the Great Organ, City Hall, Hospitals and other sights too
numerous to mention here. Trimountain, or Three Mountains,
as Boston was originally called, is a peninsula of about
700 acres, almost surrounded by the sea. Its climate in the
hottest part of seasons is deliciously cool, bracing and invigorating,
and it is undoubtedly one of the healthiest cities

THE FALL RIVER LINE
BETWEEN
NEW YORK AND BOSTON
VIA
NEWPORT AND FALL RIVER.

STEAMERS { PILGRIM AND BRISTOL. PROVIDENCE AND OLD COLONY.

THE GREAT ROUTE BETWEEN

NEW YORK AND ALL EASTERN RESORTS.

CAPE COD,
    MARTHA'S VINEYARD,
        NANTUCKET,
            WHITE MOUNTAINS,
                MOUNT DESERT, &c., &c.

Double Daily Service During Summer of 1886.

2 BOATS EVERY WEEK DAY BETWEEN

NEW YORK AND FALL RIVER.

ONE BOAT ON SUNDAY.

Splendid Bands of Music on each Boat.

Leave New York, Pier 28 North River, foot of Murray Street.

Connecting trains leave Boston from Old Colony Station, corner South and Kneeland Streets.

Annex connects to and from Brooklyn and Jersey City, only 49 miles of Rail between N. Y. and Boston. No night changes.

Send for list of Fall River line tours and copy of "**Old Colony and Pilgrim Land,**" mailed free.

GEORGE L. CONNOR,
General Passenger Agent New York.

in the world. Its harbor, one of the best on the coast, is about twenty miles long by eight wide. Its many islands and coast are lined with thousands of delightful summer resorts, reached by numerous railroads and steamboats every hour of the day, forming a panorama of busy life and pleasure to be seen nowhere else. Its drives inland are none the less interesting and picturesque, whether we visit the classic shades of old Harvard, the romantic walks at Wellesley, or the hundred delightful suburban villages, whose well-kept streets, bright lawns and elegant gardens simply reflect the elegance and taste within the homes of those who made Boston what it is. The excellent horse car service of Boston is one of the best institutions. Nowhere else in the country is this important convenience to visitors so complete as here. The broad, handsome, open cars reach all points within ten miles of the City Hall, and give visitors a most delightful opportunity to see the attractions at the least possible charge.

Boston, the capital of Massachusetts, embraces Boston proper, East Boston, South Boston, Roxbury, West Roxbury, Brighton, Charlestown and Dorchester. Boston proper, or old Boston, was very uneven in surface, and originally presenting three hills, Bacon, Copp's, the Fort, the former of which is about 130 feet above the sea. The Indian name of this peninsula was Shawmut, meaning "Sweet Waters." A narrow strip of land called the "Neck" joined the peninsula to the main land; this neck was formerly overflowed by the tide, but has been filled in and widened, and is now thickly built upon. East Boston occupies the west portion of Noodle's or Maverick's Island. Here is the deepest water of the harbor, and here the ocean steam-

If your child is lacking in the elements of perfect childhood, try Ridge's Food. It is the claim of the Manufacturers, indorsed by hundreds, that it is the best food for the growing child, we believe more children have been successfully reared upon Ridge's Food than upon all the other foods combined. Try it mothers and be convinced of its worth. Send to **WOOLRICH & CO., Palmer, Mass.,** for pamphlet. Sent free to any address. Its perusal will save much anxiety.

ers chiefly lie. The wharf now used by the Cunard steamers is 1,000 feet long. South Boston extends about two miles along the south side of the harbor, an arm of which separates it from Boston proper.

The first white inhabitant of Boston was the Rev. John Blackstone, supposed to have been an Episcopal clergyman, and to have arrived in 1623. Here he lived until 1630, when John Winthrop, (afterward the first Governor of Massachusetts) came across the river from Charlestown, where he had dwelt with some fellow immigrants for a short time. About 1635 Mr. Blackstone sold his claim to the now populous peninsula for £30, and removed to Rhode Island. The first church was built in 1632; the first wharf in 1673. Four years later a postmaster was appointed, and in 1704 (April 24th) the first newspaper, called the *Boston News Letter*, was published. The " Boston Massacre " happened March 5, 1770, when three persons were killed and five wounded by the fire of the soldiers. In 1773 tea was destroyed in the harbor, and Boston bore a conspicuous part in the opening scenes of the Revolution. The city was incorporated in 1822, with a population of 45,000, which had increased to 136,881 in 1850, to 177,850 in 1860, and 250,526 in 1870. By the recent annexation of the suburbs of Brighton, Charlestown, West Roxbury, etc., the population has been increased to 341,919 (in February, 1876). Population 362,876 in 1880. On the 9th of November, 1872, one of the most terrible conflagrations ever known in the United States swept away the principal business portion of Boston. The fire broke out on Saturday evening, and continued until noon on the following day, when it was brought under control, but again broke forth in consequence of an explosion of gas, about midnight, and raged until 7 o'clock Monday morning. The district burnt over, extended from Summer and Bedford street on the south, to near State street on the north, and from Washington street east to the harbor. About 800 of the finest buildings in the city were destroyed, causing a loss of $80,000,000.

OBJECTS OF ANTIQUARIAN INTEREST.

Among "buildings with a history," the most interesting in the United States, next to Independence Hall, in Philadelphia, is Faneuil Hall. The famous edifice, the "cradle of liberty," is in Dock Square, which also has an historical fame because of the meetings of the Revolutionary patriots that was held there. The building was erected in 1742, by Peter Faneuil, a Huguenot merchant, and by him presented to the town. Its original dimensions were 100 by 40 feet. Destroyed by fire in 1761, it was rebuilt in 1763, and enlarged to its present dimensions in 1805. A full length portrait of the founder, together with the pictures of Washington, by Stuart, of Webster, by Healey, of Samuel Adams, by Copeley, and portraits of John Quincy Adams, Edward Everett, Abraham Lincoln, and Governor Andrew adorn the walls. The basement of the hall is a market. The old State House, in Washington street, at the head of State street, was erected in 1748, and was for half a century the seat of the "Great and General Court of Massachusetts," being the building of which such frequent mention is made in revolutionary annals. It has long been given up to business purposes. the interior having been completely remodeled, and the edifice surmounted by a roof which has wholly destroyed the quaint effect of the original architecture. Christ Church (Episcopal), in Salem street, near Copp's Hill, is the oldest church in the city, having been erected in 1722. It has a lofty steeple, and in the tower is a fine chime of bells. The Old South Church, corner of Washington and Milk streets, is an object of much interest, it is of brick, and was built in 1729, on the site where the first edifice of the society had stood since 1669. The church was used as a place of meeting by the heroes of '76, and during the British occupation of the city, was used as a place for cavalry-drill. It barely escaped the flames in the great fire. The Old South Society having erected a new place of worship on Boylston street, the old building was offered for sale, when a patriotic effort among the people originated a subscription for the purpose of raising funds to secure its preservation. King's Chapel (Unitarian), corner Tremont and School streets, was founded in 1686, and the present building, a plain granite structure, erected in 1750-54. Adjoining the church is the first burying ground established in Boston. In it are buried Isaac Johnson, "the father of Boston," Governor Winthrop, John Cotton, and other distinguished men. On the corner of Washington and School streets, is the Old Corner Bookstore, a building dating from 1712. The old North Burying-ground, on the brow of Copp's Hill, was the second established in the city, and is still sacredly preserved. Here lies three fathers of the Puritan Church, Drs. Increase, Cotton and Samuel Mather.

THE OLD CEMETERY IN THE COMMON.

In that corner of the Common bounded by Tremont and Boylston streets, and lying directly between the Masonic Temple and the Public Library, is an old burying-ground, shut off from the Common and the streets by an iron fence. It was formerly known as the South, and later as the Central burying-ground. It was opened in 1756, but the oldest stone is dated 1761. The best known name upon any of the ancient stones is that of Monsieur Julien, the most noted *restaurateur* of the city a century past, and the inventor of the famous soup that still bears his name. This cemetery is the least interesting of the old burying places of Boston, and is consequently seldom noticed by the stranger.

There are according to the directory nearly two hundred hotels in the city. With that fact in view I shall mention first the American House and United States. In suggesting to intending visitors to Boston the name of the "Old United States Hotel" the proprietor feels justified in recommending the house for just what it is, no more, no less. I am at home when in the United States Hotel, it pleases me, and I am positive it will please you.

The United States Hotel is one of the oldest and best of the well-established hotels of Boston. Its fame is widespread. Its seal dates back to 1826, and from that early date to the present it has been maintained up to the best standard, but never better than now. It is situated directly opposite the Boston & Albany, within two blocks of the Old Colony, and only a short distance from the New York & New England, and Providence Railroad Stations, and is the nearest hotel to the retail portions of the city, and the great commercial centres.

The "United States" is occupied largely in winter by families owning their own private residences in the adjoining towns, who come into the city and make their residence at this famous old house for the winter months. During the summer season, therefore, their great family rooms are available for tourists, families, and pleasure parties, giving accommodations that could not otherwise be afforded, and so allow guests the most extensive variety of rooms at the low est possible charges. During the summer months the rates are reduced to $2.50, $3.00, and $3.50 per day, according to accommodations, with board ; rooms without board $1.00 and upwards, thus giving visitors an opportunity of making this hotel their permanent headquarters, from which to make daily excursions to the thousand places of historical interest with which the city and suburbs abound, and to the great manufacturing cities which surround it ; while the fifteen hundred summer resorts and boarding-houses down the harbor and along the coast are available every fifteen minutes by boat or rail. Thus the " United States " will be found

AMERICAN HOUSE
BOSTON.

✥ Central Location, Perfect Ventilation. ✥

UNEXCEPTIONABLE TABLE.

THE NEAREST

FIRST=CLASS HOTEL

TO NORTHERN AND EASTERN DEPOTS.

Particularly Desirable for Families and Tourists. Conveniently Located for either Business or Pleasure.

American Plan, $3.00 per DAY and upwards
Rooms only   1.00 "   "   "   "   "
According to Size and Location of Room.

PARLORS AND BATHS EXTRA.

REFITTED AND GREATLY IMPROVED.
BY RECENT ALTERATIONS.

HENRY B. RICE & Co., Proprietors.
Hanover, near Washington St.

not only a most accessible and convenient hotel on arriving at Boston, but will be found equally comfortable and economical for permanent as well as transient guests, while the facilities for reaching all the suburban localities and various sea-shore resorts are unequalled by any hotel in Boston.

The American House, Boston, is the nearest first-class hotel to the Northern and Eastern Railroad Depots, and can without hesitation, be recommended as one of the best in the city. It has broad, well lighted corridors, spacious public rooms and all modern improvements for the convenience of guests, and has long been noted for the cleanliness and comfort of its rooms, the invariable excellence of its table, and that air of home-like comfort which is so refreshing to the tired traveler. It has a large number of suites particulary desirable for families and large parties, and contains no dark rooms in which to store away an unsuspecting midnight guest. It is perfectly ventilated, has six stairways from top to bottom, and recently renovated and improved; furnishes superior accommodations at more moderate rates than most first-class hotels. It is regularly kept on the American plan, charging $3.00 and $3.50 per day, according to size and location of rooms, and is deservedly popular with the best class of pleasure and commercial travelers, but rooms are let with or without meals at the option of guests.

One of the best traveling companions on a pleasure trip is a reliable Railway Guide, and we advise the tourist to get the best, as a cheap guide is like a cheap watch—never on time.

As we hold that this little volume is not thrown away, but taken home for future reference, a little advice of how to start upon a trip, &c., would not come amiss. We say

1st, Select your route. 2d, Buy your tickets and secure your parlor car seats. 3d, Show your tickets to the baggage master and have your baggage checked. 4th, Go to the news stand and ask for The "Phat Boy's" Racy Description of the St. Lawrence River, or the Pathfinder's Railway Guide, as it is the oldest railway guide published, and the July number will contain the best railroad map ever published. It is the only recognized mouthpiece of the Passenger Agents Association; one can be assured of its reliability. The Phat Boy requests his friends to send to them next spring for a copy of their summer tours to select your vacation trip. Address, Pathfinder, Boston, Mass. 5th, Don't bother the conductor by asking questions, as he has all he can do to attend to his train, and the Pathfinder's official tables and valuable maps tell the whole story.

I have endeavored to describe faithfully and correctly the route over which you have passed, dear reader. There are, doubtless, some whose knowledge of particular points is greater than my own ; to those I say most cheerfully, note them down, and forward to me, 21 Chestnut Park, Rochester, N. Y., and, I assure you, they shall have a position in the next edition of this work, as my object and aim is to make this a perfect guide for any person desirous of making this, the finest trip on the continent.

After returning home and resuming the cares and position which you left behind for this trip, may you be filled with animation, life and health acquired by your excursion trip down the St. Lawrence, etc., and the pleasant memories of scenes witnessed, wonders visited, as well as the beauties of nature revealed, you will have double the vigor to prosecute the duties devolving upon you, with only spare time on hand to speak to your acquaintances and friends, recommending them to make the same trip, not forgetting to mention The " Phat Boy's" Racy Description of the St. Lawrence River as a guide for hotel and all points of interest connected with the trip. I will now lift my hat to the tourist and others who have made the trip, and bid them a temporary farewell. Hoping to see, next vacation yourself and friends, I only say

ADIEU.

WM. S. KIMBALL & CO.,
ROCHESTER, N. Y.

FRAGRANT VANITY FAIR,

SUPERLATIVE,

CLOTH OF GOLD,

STRAIGHT CUT CIGARETTES.

People of refined taste who desire exceptionally fine Cigarettes should use only our Straight Cut, put up in Satin Packets and Boxes of

10s, 20s, 50s, and 100s.

www.ingramcontent.com/pod-product-compliance
Lightning Source LLC
Chambersburg PA
CBHW020251170426
43202CB00008B/326